D0533775

THE ABSOLUTE SECRET

THE ABSOI JTE SECRET

Beyond the suffering ...he key to inner peace

Raymond Phelan

JANUS PUBLISHING COMPANY
London, England

First published in Great Britain 2009
by Janus Publishing Company Ltd,
105–107 Gloucester Place,
London W1U 6BY

www.januspublishing.co.uk

British Library Cataloguing-in-Publication Data
A catalogue record for this book is available from the British Library

ISBN 978-1-85756-765-6

Cover Design: Edwin Page

Printed and bound in Great Britain

Dedicated to you, the reader,
and to seekers of truth and self-knowledge everywhere.
May the divine heart
be the expression and fulfilment of your life.

God's plan is to make known his secret
to his people, this rich and glorious secret
which he has for all peoples.
And the secret is that Christ is in you,
which means that you will share
in the glory of God.

(Colossians 1:27)

Acknowledgements

I wish to thank all those people and situations that have come into my life as lessons and those who offered their kind words of wisdom, guidance, love and support while this book was being produced, and to Mary Lacey with whom the idea for this book was first discussed. I would particularly like to thank Kathy Smale for her enduring patience and endless hours of dedication to the typing and preparation of the final manuscripts.

To all my 'Eccles Street' friends and TMers – thank you for being there – and, of course, I would especially like to thank my two early mentors, both of whom fundamentally influenced me, in their separate ways, as regards to the spiritual aspect of life: Dr Tony Quinn, thank you – and with deepest respects to His Holiness Maharishi Mahesh Yogi; Jai Guru Dev.

A Space

I've found a place, so deep inside,
a space where peace just never hides,
where love it flows, and my heart knows
that this is heaven I've been shown;
a space where time and tears all end,
a state when my soul it transcends,
my heart reflects the love it feels,
there's nothing more that it could need.

Contents

Preface

For ye were sometimes darkness,
but now are ye light in the Lord:
walk as children of light:
(For the fruit of the Spirit is in all goodness
and righteousness and truth;)

(Ephesians 5:8–9)

Many people who start to practice meditation do so out of a need to be free of some kind of personal suffering or stress. I can assure the reader that for me, this was no exception – with heartache and suffering real and acute, reaching my lowest point many times. And yet, the lowest point of not being able to take any more, when it just felt that there must be more to life, was the catalyst, the miracle, that changed my life for the good. After many unsuccessful journeys down the conventional route of doctors and medication I sought the spiritual solution to peace of mind. One day, a chink of light appeared in the form of an advertisement for meditation and on reading a 'good news only' paper for the first time, following which a surge of nature within empowered my soul, born of the necessity for change and soul evolution. The 'more to life' had begun.

I took the plunge into learning about meditation, but this at first was a kind of stop-go affair in which my practice was irregular. Then I attended healing therapy classes and I went on spiritual mind-expanding seminars, all of which I loved and found really beneficial. Then, on another 'one day', I had another surge of nature's prompt: it became clear that the practice of daily mantra meditation was definitely the way of life for me. Although initiated nearly thirty years ago, the last twenty years or so of twice daily meditation has become the most central feature of my life and it has totally transformed me as a person.

Although well-intentioned, dedicated and hard-working, some religions these days seem to be floundering, with interest and attendance dwindling and questions often asked as to their effectiveness in today's world. The spirit needs to be brought back into them, via the people, who are 'the rock' of religions. Places of worship are, indeed, holy and sacred, but it is the individuals that house the spirit within themselves. Through the people, this spirit needs to be brought forth in a more practical, experiential and expressive manner. Meditation is not intended here as a substitute for religious practice, but rather as a way to enhance it. A service of worship should be a joyful, loving, spiritual occasion; a devotional period with the divine, a celebration of life, and I believe daily meditation to be a means to this end.

The purpose of this book is to help raise people's consciousness from the quagmire of personal suffering, because there is no need any more for ignorance and misery. So to all seekers of peace, love, health and prosperity, through spirituality, I salute your courage to break free from the bondage of societal-consciousness: the conditioned mind. Your courage will be rewarded.

To Heaven My Tears Cry Out

When each step seems like a desert trek
of highway to be crossed,
when the journey there before me
can feel like I am lost,
when on days things seem beyond me
like an endless friendless road,
and sometimes like an island
I feel so all alone,

When the seasons cease their pleasin'
and love has lost its shade,
when each day seems like a roundabout
of circles I have made,
when emotions of the heart cry out
my reservoir to fill,
when the thirst for love is greater
than all the world can give,

When the tide of life is flowing wild
upon the sea of time,
when each wide and weary mile seems like
an ocean out of rhyme,
when it's raining from a cloudless sky
and night-time knows no day,
when the meadows and the summer fields
reflect a shade of grey,

It's to heaven my tears cry out
for His arms to comfort me,
for that reassuring hug of love
I plead so earnestly,
that He keeps right on just holding,
enfolding like a breeze,
oh, His love it is, for the peace it gives,
the only thing I need.

Success

So get rid of your old self,
which made you live as you used to –
the old self that was being destroyed by its deceitful desires.
Your hearts and minds must be made completely new,
(Ephesians 4:22–23)

For most people nowadays success is measured strictly from the materialistic standpoint and is relative to their possessions. They would include as the criteria things like a large, fancy house, with a swimming pool, a couple of new cars in a long sweeping driveway and, of course, the perfect relationship. Winning the lotto jackpot also seems to be most people's dream answer to success and happiness. There is nothing wrong with aspirations of abundance; after all, Jesus promised it to us and the Bible has its fair share of millionaires, but this so-called success so often turns out to be just a richer, wealthier style of misery, disillusionment and suffering. For instance, how many millionaires in Hollywood and other places of glitz, glamour and fame are truly happy with this success. I would suggest very few.

So what is real success and how can it be defined in ourselves and others? What are its characteristics, its outward signs, its nature? Surely a bank balance or social standing isn't the barometer that determines this. If that were the case, then all those millionaires would portray luminous characteristics, they would seem to be extremely joyful and contented, but sadly this is not so for, in fact, their misery tends to match in proportion to their bank balance. But, as the Bible says, what good is your wealth if in gaining it you lose your soul, your conscious awareness of your true nature, and you become taken over by attachments and illusory desires?

So what is the solution? Jesus said, 'I come that you may have Life, and have it in abundance'. He not only means that we can have material and financial wealth, to be used wisely for the comfort of ourselves and others, and an abundance of God-given talents, skills and ideas to employ creatively for the greater good of the world, but, more importantly, spiritual abundance.

Before chasing fame and fortune it would be wise to consider these words of scripture, 'First seek the Kingdom, then everything else shall be added', 'The Kingdom of God is within', 'Be still and know that I am God'. These words sum it all up for me, simply and perfectly. Although expressed slightly differently, the message is the same; to raise our consciousness from the ordinary to the divine – then watch the magic unfold. We will then be able to recognise that real wealth and abundance – real success – is primarily spiritual. The purpose of human life is to give birth to divine life, the nature of which is bliss, which is inner peace, love, perfect health and abundance of all that is good. That is why we are to 'first seek the Kingdom', so that our success is divinely inspired, benefiting and sustaining not only ourselves, but others also.

The way to seek the kingdom is through the practice of meditation and in doing so, as we become more and more purified of heart and mind, our state of being evolves into one of detachment; a sense of easing back from the great effort to be materialistic as a means of happiness, fulfilment and success. We no longer rate our success from this perspective or consider our possessions our source of contentment.

Prior to this enlightenment, our possessions were actually a source of bondage. We were addicted to the material world for our enjoyment, even sometimes being devastated at the loss of certain possessions. We need to be aware that relying on these outside things to define ourselves, for our sense of security and worth, will result in sorrow and anxiety if we lose them. This is contrary to spiritual law, to God's law – it is without substance, a shadow, ephemeral, illusory. The only genuine, authentic source of real and lasting happiness and contentment – success – that hasn't been brought about is the kingdom within. So our primary goal must be to first seek the kingdom, or self-realisation, meaning become fully integrated beings rising from human-consciousness, through cosmic-consciousness, to God-consciousness; 'Man is made in the image and likeness of God'.

Through our meditation practice, our human-consciousness becomes transformed into divine-consciousness and our dependency on material possessions and addictions for our success fades away as we realise that the true source of everything real and lasting is within raised consciousness. Meditation enlarges the conscious capacity of the mind, like the submerged four-fifths of the iceberg integrating with the one-fifth that is above the water. As St Peter said, 'That we come into the full stature of Christ'. We now feel free to enjoy our possessions while they are there, without the need to obsessively own or depend on them as a means of measuring our success.

This also applies to personal relationships. We shouldn't try to own or manipulate the other, but rather promote and encourage their freedom from within their consciousness, while still loving each other, allowing the other to grow and develop as a spiritual being. We do not depend on each other as our only source of happiness and love, but we enjoy a sharing and giving process, rather than a taking and storing one. Everything is seen in the light of joint integration, like contributing to a non-egocentric neutral pool, which either party can draw from without feeling compromised. By supporting each other's spiritual growth we experience our own true inner essence – bliss – more deeply and profoundly and this is reflected back to the other, into their world. The purpose of a relationship is to inspire each other to give birth to their inner self, their true nature of spiritual love, and thus raise the consciousness of mankind.

With the absence of such spiritual awareness it is hardly surprising then to note the number of 'failed' marriages and relationships in recent years, particularly in the so-called 'well-off' society of 'successful' people in the business, political and entertainment world. They 'fail' because both parties are not rooted in a spiritually evolving awareness. Sometimes, couples get together through mere physical attraction only and although the sex and the wild nights on the town may be exciting, sooner or later this false flame of passion, that is sourced from without and not within, will burn itself out or become an addiction. The perceived happiness or success image diminishes and the union is no longer fulfilling. Much conflict ensues and parting is inevitable. Such a relationship is simply a battery-type, gross, meaningless affair, whereas if it were based on a sound spiritual footing, in conscious contact with the divine – real love – then it would flourish.

For success and happiness in relationships it is vital that both are coming from the same base of spiritual understanding; a spirit-to-spirit relationship whereby each are experiencing authentic love. Then our unenlightened consciousness becomes awakened to bliss. Each should encounter the other's essence from their own hallowed state of pure, unconditional love that emerges through the heart and not the unintegrated ego, which contaminates, distorts and clouds with judgements, prejudices and opinions. Both parties acknowledge the divinity of the other and in this way, it is a real love-to-love affair, as in 'Love thy neighbour as thy Self', which is also the way we meet everybody else, of course, be it family, friend or stranger. Our higher self is pure love, so first we are just to 'be', just to love, unconditionally, and see everyone through that raised consciousness.

It is the natural instinctive urge, the evolutionary path, of the spirit to guide all to inner peace and spiritual success. Even though one may be going through suffering, which is the re-enactment of the conditioned state, the heart and mind are crying out to be made whole, to be made fully conscious of the already present divine state within. This is achieved through the inner silence of meditation.

Let us not confuse this goal of attaining inner peace – spiritual success – with the journey. The goal is already in place within each person; we don't have to create it; God is the goal and He is waiting for our conscious contact, so that our divine nature can be experienced and expressed. We only have to commence the journey; the goal is assured. The direction of this journey is inwards and the process we use is meditation. It all starts with a deliberate decision on our part to be taught how and then to practice daily, leading us to follow the 'royal' road to bliss-consciousness, self-realisation, where the journey becomes interwoven with the goal.

The secret of spiritual success is to learn the technique of meditation and to continue with this practice daily. This way we will let our life unfold naturally, in the divine way that God intended, loving all situations non-judgementally and without resistance as they evolve. We are compassionate in all our interpersonal dealings and relationships and we strive for the kingdom, for self-realisation, that alone provides the deep inner peace and contentment, the joy that we are all seeking. This is the beginning of the end of suffering and misery, the road to happiness of heart and success at the art of living. 'And I, if I be raised shall draw all men unto Me', sums up spiritual success beautifully. The word 'man' in the Bible often means 'man'ifestation – God is cause, man is effect, so in the quote; when we raise our consciousness we shall draw forth all God's manifestations – love, peace, health, prosperity, and abundance; we see, hear, and feel, communicate and express, from the divine spirit. This is true success.

Heaven of My Being

Life bids us many tidings
as we journey, everyone,
and always life is guiding
to know of peace and love;
Oh, the peace I heard spoke silently,
it led me to within,
while the space therein announced to me:
surrender and be still.

Life journeys many highways,
some longwinding and uphill,
yet life gives many choices
and its voice it is free will;
Oh, along the way life it did sow
its message to be still,
silent wisdom from where to grow
in His kingdom and His will.

Life is the silent teacher,
its tutors all around,
and life sometimes will take us where
the lessons can be found;
But of all the meanings I've been shown
this one I can't forget,
it's that journey that has taken me
to the space where love I met.

For this space I've known, it takes me home
to where I've been searching for,
loving feelings so revealing
that my soul it search no more;
And from this depth of quietness
came the truth of inner seeing,
a silence leading me to know
the heaven of my being.

Happiness

Know ye not that ye are the temple of God,
and that the Spirit of God dwelleth in you?
(I Corinthians 3:16)

The purpose of our life is to become 'realised' beings – this is our first priority. We must each develop bliss-consciousness in order to know true happiness. God's intention for us is to have heaven now – while on earth. Without exception, the innate yearning of every human being is the seeking of happiness; to experience, on a moment-to-moment basis, the state of love within; that blissful happiness which endows us with an irrepressible smile, that inner glow of contentment and peace.

Like salmon heading upstream to fulfil their life's purpose and evolution, we are each intuitively driven to find this happiness, this bliss. It is something that we suspect is somewhere out there and possible to attain. Regrettably, some of us seek it through unnatural means, sadly to our cost, while others stay rooted in the past, in a fixed state of illusion, seemingly content in misery; a strange paradox, indeed.

So what must we do to attain this happiness? Many of us try to provide ourselves with it by way of material possessions and while this may seem to work in the short term, sooner or later it wears off and more and more worldly goods are needed to top up the initial effect. After a while that sort of layering of 'conditional material happiness' becomes like a bottomless pit, from which we never seem to attain that particular 'thing' that totally fulfils us. We may also interpret random happy moments as true happiness, but these are not the same. Happy moments can be fleeting, are relative, whereas true happiness, being spiritual, is of a permanent nature.

The ego gets used to being overfed and pampered and it doesn't take kindly to having its meals taken away, much like taking a bone from a dog! The ego is not interested in sincere, radiant smiles or natural happiness and freedom. It will always have demands, a list of goodies that need to be supplied, an acquisitive ransom if you like, for this covenant of material happiness to be satisfactorily maintained. But this quest for happiness through the ego is illusory, rooted in fear and addiction, surviving through ignorance and suppression in the subconscious, an unceasing trek of keeping up with keeping up.

The same can be said of personal suffering, where we are prepared to just accept our problem, whereby it is sustained in a similar way as with the material addiction. Some of us have blocked things out to the degree that the mere mention of happiness upsets us, because this reminds us of what is possible by a change of mindset, and it makes us feel guilty. But we still moan about our lot to anyone who will listen, usually another moaner, creating a sort of moany-go-round club, which keeps the unhappiness alive and gives it a dynamic. To speak of love, bliss and happiness is like a joke or fiction, even scary, and almost enough to cause offence: 'How dare you speak of happiness to me!'

We are so familiar with the conditioned way that we may think our unhappiness is justified – for example, by an event or situation – and therefore acceptable; a normal way to live. But God did not create suffering or distress, He has to be found and lived for happiness to be our experience. The mere thinking of happiness will not provide happiness; we need to live it through our consciousness; develop love-consciousness. This is God's intention for each of us – that we journey to the Promised Land, to the kingdom of heaven, to self-realisation. Happiness that isn't sourced through God is not true happiness.

So where is this happiness to be found? Well, the good Lord in His wisdom, knowing how such a precious gift could be lost, decided to place it where it would be safe, yet easily found: He placed it within us, within our consciousness – 'The Kingdom of God is Within'. So the secret is no longer a secret; the secret of happiness lies within! It was always there and always will be. It is eternally dormant within us, regardless of our situation or material or financial wealth, just like an oilfield awaiting exploration. It is our purpose in life to discover and express it.

Another analogy is that this happiness within is like the sun, which may be obscured by clouds, but above and behind the clouds is ever beaming, glowing, shining, smiling, just waiting for the gap in the clouds for it to shine through. The clouds are our thoughts and the gap is the silence between the thoughts when our minds become still. In meditation, this silence grows and expands, allowing the experience of love and happiness into our minds and hearts. This gap between our thoughts, between the incessant thinking and rethinking, allows a spark of 'sunshine' to be kindled within our heart, within our consciousness. The continual conveyor belt of mental chatter causes our inner 'sunshine' to be shrouded, our smiles to be frowns, our bliss nature to be blighted. Through meditation, a divine spark within is ignited, presently exploding into happiness and bliss.

Normal physical activity is essential after practising meditation in order for the nervous system and senses to become purified and transformed, as these need to become 'acclimatised' to withstand the nature of divine happiness. Water takes the shape of every pipe, but first the pipe has to be unclogged. Once we have a clear flow of divine expression then happiness is right on cue: like a deep undercurrent, it permeates our being; a behind-the-scenes force silently pulsating, perceived by us as well-being, contentment, inner peace, joy and loving goodwill that keeps us smiling within our hearts.

We were not created to crawl in the gloom of unhappiness; we were meant to fly in spirit. Just one ray of sunshine and the darkness of night is over as dawn breaks. This dawn signifies our second birth, our real birth – our resurrection from the dead – from the psychic sleep of ignorance, from the mire, from the suffering state of the subconscious mind, where all misery is stored. By expressing the nature of this dawn, thus are we elevated from unhappiness to divine happiness and bliss.

Time to Grow

Oh, love is such a joy, a wonder to live by,
its happiness forever flowing freely;
a tide that keeps us right, its wave makes all things bright,
and it flows into the world through you and me.

And like an open wing, released unto the wind,
love reaches out in such uplifting ways;
this beauty we are a part, the journey of the heart,
yes, love makes all things lighter in our day.

There comes a time for us, when change it is a must,
to shed old ways, to seek a brighter morn,
a time for us to grow, a time for letting go,
a time for us to sow a brand new dawn.

Let's take the time to know, let's see how rivers flow,
such peacefulness they echo, oh so clearly,
round every rock 'n stone, they flow in loving tone,
there's nothing that will keep them from the sea.

There comes a time for us, on the road of life we must,
like rivers we are asked to sparkle bright,
though clouds they may appear, love overcomes all fear,
there's nothing that will keep us from the light.

Fish Out of Water

Then we shall no longer be children,
carried by the waves
and blown about by every shifting wind
of the teaching of deceitful men,
who lead others into error by the tricks they invent.
(Ephesians 4:14)

We exist in an ocean of bliss-consciousness, in an ocean of abundance, of all that our hearts desire, yet many of us do not realise it and we behave like a 'fish out of water', even insisting on asking other fish if they could spare a glass of water or accepting glasses of water proffered to us.

Society at large tends to be like that, trying to obtain small portions of conditional pleasure or gain from wherever or whoever is offering it. For example, if it comes from another fish then it must be the real thing – sparkling and uncontaminated. Surely there cannot be any harm in asking for or taking a drink of water from another fish; is it not only water, after all?

Advertisements from all quarters of corporate mankind are constantly offering us 'glasses of contaminated water' via products and services, which many feel will 'quench their thirst' or give them fulfilment, but which in actual fact, in most cases, definitely will not. Most of these products, the ones that need regular exposure, will be of no benefit to a person's overall mental, physical and spiritual development. We must never forget that, as spiritual beings, not everything offered to us by corporate mankind is for our greater good, particularly if those offering the 'water' are not of a spiritual nature.

If we are living from an unrealised state of awareness, then we're like fish out of water; we will always be seeking out someone else's water, someone else's idea or form of pleasure, from whatever source. We then get to like it and very soon, what once seemed a harmless drink of water from a seemingly reputable source now turns into a tsunami of suffering. Through our ignorance of truth within, through the non-experiencing of our true nature, untold hardship ensues.

But why, you may ask, didn't someone tell us of this hidden danger? Why were we not notified of this potential threat to our health and well-being, this offer of illusion for reality? But we were; it is just that we didn't understand what they were talking about, it wasn't explained in simple, everyday, ABC language and besides, they would make no profit if we were spiritual and happy! This way, through democratic greed, we have to keep going back for more unclean, impure water, more quick fixes. We aspire more and more to getting deeper and deeper into the mire of misery, which satisfies the profit margins of the corporate nescience with their 'couldn't care less' mentality.

This reckless approach by corporate mankind, through their indiscriminate advertising, of offering to their fellow man and woman that seemingly innocuous 'drink of water', was never more apparent than in TV 'soap operas'. These are cleverly written and crafted to have maximum emotional impact. The themes of such programmes keep us firmly fixed, via the storylines of the day, on alcohol, cigarettes, pharmaceuticals, gambling, even sex and violence, and other mood-altering products and activities. The entertainment value of these dramas may be good, you could say, but they carry highly addictive subliminal messages from many fronts. But that is their function, their purpose; to get us 'hooked', either on the 'water' (the product) or the storylines, each reinforcing the other.

But, of course, once we're aware of the ploy of these 'soaps' we can be on our guard. Now you have been warned. Now you know the tactics they are using to take over your mind. The point being, notice where your attention is while watching TV, listening to the radio or simply looking at billboards. Watch out for that 'drink of water' being offered to you for your so-called good, health and enjoyment and understand how you or your children are being programmed and conditioned from the agendas and mindsets of others.

The secret of learning a musical instrument is called spaced repetition: play it, leave it, have a rest, do something else, play it again, leave it, etc. This pattern conditions the brain and this is precisely how advertising works to condition us over a period of time about a product. After a short while we can sing the advert off by heart or remember trigger words or phrases. The advertiser's job is to manipulate and condition our minds, to grab our unrealised state through the use of current and topical issues that we can relate to, because it is then that our five senses are unprotected and exposed to the ravages of corporate greed. This is how addictions set in with the resulting hell that follows. The onus is on us to take the precautions to ensure that this doesn't happen to us through the various media of advertising.

When a person is living through ignorance of truth, the unrealised state of awareness, their mind, their senses and their entire nervous system are at the mercy of the conditioned pleasure-seeking senses, because the five senses are duty-bound to provide the mind with pleasure, from wherever or whatever source that may come. It is the function of the five senses to provide as much pleasure to the mind as possible. The mind that has not made conscious contact with the inner spirit is called the unrealised mind, which will not argue, because it is ever seeking more and more pleasure and happiness of any nature. This will continue until the mind wakes up to its true nature, which is bliss-consciousness. The so-called pleasure that the mind seeks is really repetitive addiction, which has rooted itself in, and then becomes part of, what is known as the subconscious mind. It is like a vicious circle of automated programming, caused through conditioning of the mind and senses while in the state of ignorance, through constant exposure to and intake of unnatural sources of 'happiness'.

So how can we protect ourselves from those who wish to take over our minds? The answer is simple: learn the art of meditation and experience the inner strength and natural happiness gained by making conscious contact with the inner spirit. Through regular practice a purification process takes place and addictive patterns are eliminated.

The subconscious mind, which housed all that conditioning, becomes fully conscious and awake to the experience of spiritual love and bliss. This heightened awareness then protects us from harmful influences.

Consider the Bible story of David and Goliath: David the shepherd boy slew Goliath the giant with his white marble, which he carried with him everywhere in his breast pocket. This white marble was David's state of enlightenment, his present-moment awareness. He took out this 'white light' and slung it towards the giant (the underlying problem), and felled the beast, meaning light overcame darkness. Darkness cannot prevail over the Christ-light awareness, which is within us all. But the light needs activating, which occurs through meditation, so then we become as David and we let no-one succeed in persuading us to accept their 'glass of water' or overcome us the way Goliath tried to with David.

Prior to self-realisation, while still in the desert state of ignorance, our senses, like antennae, are tuned only to receive according to their level of purity. During meditation our senses automatically withdraw inwards, like a tortoise retreating into its shell, to allow for the process of purification to take place. This is how, afterwards, the senses emerge cleansed and heightened, ready to protect the mind spiritually, to serve us holistically, to serve the kingdom. The result of regular meditation is life experienced in freedom from addiction. Our free will is redeemed and we reach the Promised Land. The divine angler rescues us from the stagnant pool. He restores and reconnects our spirit, for it to grow and expand even greater, as He intended – 'and even greater things shall ye do'. We are spiritual beings, truly living in His ocean of bliss-consciousness, no longer in the cesspool of conditioning, seeking out a pittance of illusory and temporary pleasures and dodgy 'glasses of water!'

Freedom

Sound of freedom, echoed stillness,
laughter pitch in children's play,
unmeasured time, unending space,
creative now fulfilling dreams.

Pure awareness, state of being,
reflective daylight of my spirit,
playground of the child within,
aged wisdom's abiding home.

Mountain bloom, wild in peace,
unhindered beauty's touching presence,
captured love's releasing scent,
hostage of my heart's desire.

Journey in the Spirit tongue,
nourished word communicating,
language of the rooted silence,
depthful space proclaiming peace.

Summer wings in golden space,
germ of truth in present moment,
guiding breeze within a storm,
openness through inner calm.

Majestic flight of eagle's prayer,
gliding life's evolving currents,
flowing with the breath of love,
childlike state of freedom's heart.

The Process

Give ear to my words O Lord,
consider my meditation.
Hearken unto the voice of my cry, my King, and my God:
for unto thee will I pray.

(Psalm 5:1–2)

Meditation is an ancient art which predates all major religions, including Christianity. It is one of the most important practices we can carry out, as it is life-changing and transformational, the secret of overall health, well-being, deep inner peace, happiness and prosperity. Missing out on daily meditation is forgoing the opportunity of effortlessly coming into conscious contact with inner bliss, love and God.

To the ordinary man and woman, bliss may be but a pie in the sky, Eastern holy word describing some intellectual, unreachable state. Yet, it is our reality. It is deep within our consciousness, it is our true nature and it can be experienced by everyone. There are many forms of meditation, but they should all lead to mind expansion. Meditation is both the practice and the outcome, for it can be understood as 'I am sitting down meditating' and afterwards as 'I am now living my life as a reflection of it; this is my new way of life'.

Meditation is unification of heart and mind, integration of subconscious and conscious, one expanding into the other. Hence, 'expanded consciousness', which is the state of awareness whereby we give conscious permission, instead of automatic unconscious permission, to our actions. The state of ignorance of our true nature is the cause of all suffering or sin and it is the programmed and conditioned subconscious mind that creates this state.

The practice of meditation is simple, consisting merely of thinking of a mantra, which is a repeated sound or vibration in word form. The use of a mantra allows the conscious mind to settle down and it stops it wandering into daydreams or compulsively thinking about anything and everything, which is the activity of an undisciplined mind. The mantra stills the conscious mind sufficiently to enable the body and all its inner mechanisms, the breath and the nervous system to become utterly relaxed, releasing the build-up of stress. The breathing becomes refined, gentle and deep and the nervous system reaches a state of restful alertness, where it is neither active nor passive. This state is key to the experience of bliss. It takes a little time to become acclimatised or 'at home' in this mental stillness, but the benefits in terms of overall health and spiritual growth are enormous. Meditation is simple, but it is utter and complete surrender, where intuitively we know that we are engaged in a right and natural practice that is safe and that God, in His almighty power, is guiding the process.

One of the things we notice when we commence practising meditation is the amount of thoughts that come up in our minds, but the secret is to leave them alone. Not to try to get rid of them, to try to become thoughtless, but just to ignore them and not to engage in their nature. We are not the author of these thoughts as long as we don't deliberately bring them up to think about. They are transient thoughts, which will just come and go once we don't 'deal' with them or acknowledge them; to do this we just gently return to our mantra.

When using the mantra during meditation we are 'thinking' it, but not 'thinking about' it. Translated, the word 'mantra' means 'mind protection', so it protects the mind from straying by anchoring it in present-moment awareness, which is the opposite of the illusory past and future states of mind that so many are addicted to. We are preoccupied with this, choosing through ignorance to live in the past, re-enacting situations formed in the subconscious mind, relating to them almost like present-day reality, not knowing how to get off this repetitive 'thinking about' treadmill. This will continue until we set about a mind expansion programme, such as meditation. Because the past and future are not present-moment reality, we can never find authentic awareness or bliss there. This can only be experienced in 'now' consciousness.

Sometimes, we might 'meditate' on a situation or problem in our life. This has its value in the sense of looking more closely at it, contemplating and evaluating the options and deciding on a plan of action, which seems to offer a solution, but it is really only as useful as moving the furniture around in a foggy room. True meditation is quite different. It is a practice whereby we are most definitely not pondering over any situation or problem, or seeking solutions or insights. Instead, we are totally surrendering our struggles or whatever the discomfort may be, letting go of the 'hands-on' involvement of our human finite mind, trying intellectually to resolve whatever it may be, be it personal, local, national or global.

We mistakenly believe that our own limited, deluded mind can regulate and manipulate God, the author of the universe and the evolutionary process. As if one tiny raindrop by itself alone can produce a tidal wave without the power of the ocean! Having said that, it is possible to misuse or abuse the creative power for a time, but evolution will always correct this and the evolution of each individual soul to its full divine status will always come about eventually – when the soul has had enough suffering.

The nature of man is twofold: we are each relative and absolute simultaneously. In other words, we each carry heaven within our physicality. The seed of heaven is already within us, within our consciousness, although it may not as yet be experiential to us. We are intended to give birth to this seed, to our heavenly state while on earth, so that we may live in heaven on earth.

During meditation, our relative aspects – meaning our physicality, intellect, egos, desires and intentions – are all relinquished to the mantra. This suspension of our relative state, our effort, allows our mind to come under the influence of our absolute state or heavenly state, giving birth to our eternal self or self-realisation. This is transcendental bliss being infused into the very nature of the mind, the integration of the finite mind into infinite mind, heaven into earth, meaning bliss is heaven and we are earth. Like nail to magnet, it is union with God.

Meditation is not about shrinking from or evading our duties and responsibilities, but rather an opportunity to unplug from our addictive thoughts, 'leave our muddy boots outside the door', leave outside our opinions, attitudes, likes, dislikes and worries. 'Before ye enter the Temple, forgive', and enter a neutral zone, a deep inner silence, peace and freedom from the slavery of that wasteful, tiresome, 'thinking about'. We cannot bring the ego into the transcendent. Afterwards, what we left outside is hardly recognisable and we resume our daily lives from a fresh perspective, attending to our duties and responsibilities more effectively with new awareness and understanding.

This is purification, integration, bringing the heart and mind together into harmony and balance, the transformation of the nervous system to the level where it can sustain bliss. 'In my Father's Kingdom there are many mansions', means that for each level of consciousness there is a corresponding level within the nervous system.

The state of bliss is our real true nature, which is lost to us through stress and unhealthy lifestyles, the conditioned state, the subconscious mind, formed through ignorance when we denied present-moment awareness and hid ourselves from God. The subconscious mind contains all our past thought seeds, which dictate our future actions, good or bad. We reap what we sow. It is like a perfectly mastered CD that contains all our behavioural programming, beliefs, views and limitations. The more we listen to this CD, the more we validate and grow the contents, allowing them to overpower and defeat us. If we are not in good physical and mental health and if we are not living a life of prosperity, then we are obviously under the influence of that CD, the subconscious, conditioned state.

This keeps a person, even a country, rooted in personal or national hardship and misery. Any happiness is contrived and artificial, a short-lived surge effect, with mood fluctuations. It is like functioning from batteries instead of the mains. Being connected to our source, 'the mains', and not operating from conditioning, will keep us vibrant and youthful, perpetually optimistic and happy.

Meditation brings us to a natural and more fulfilling spiritual happiness which, in turn, affects our health beneficially. Without any effort on our part, the heart, the five senses and the entire nervous system automatically undergo a natural rejuvenation, a process of purification, as in 'It is not I who do the healing but my Father which is in Heaven'. The good gardener, to affect the health of the whole tree, will water the roots not the leaves, so meditation is like watering our consciousness, to affect our whole health and happiness.

At some point during meditation we transcend our relative state and enter expanded consciousness, so we experience union with divine-consciousness, our true nature, bliss. At this time we are no longer experiencing through our five senses and afterwards, with them having been heightened spiritually, we perceive life from this new level of sensory awareness, in which we see and hear from the heart, as in 'He healed the blind and the deaf'. In other words, we become fully conscious cosmic beings, living and expressing our true nature of love, peace and prosperity, thus eliminating the subconscious state of ignorance forever.

Meditation grounds and roots us in present-moment bliss and ignorance of this consciousness is costly in terms of health, happiness and spiritual growth. The unrealised mind is in constant need of junk diets, TV and news, which keeps it dull, fatigued and non-creative, so it is essential that our nervous system and our senses be, as it were, unplugged from all of this to allow for healing and restoration. We cannot progress to a higher level of consciousness while still holding on to a lower level by continuing that lifestyle. We cannot bring darkness into light, but we can bring light into darkness. To have sparkling health, a sharp mind and inner peace and contentment, it is vital to shift our consciousness from living intellectually to living from the transcendent. In order for bliss to become our permanent state of being, it is necessary that, after our meditation, we express its nature out into the world. This roots our consciousness in bliss.

If we plant weeds in our garden, more weeds are produced. So it is with our mind – whatever we keep thinking will be produced in our lives. 'Ask and ye shall receive'. The nature of our thoughts forms the nature of our reality. We reap what we sow. Our subconscious or conditioned mind is a collection of perennial weeds. Meditation removes these weeds and replaces them with flowers, transforming our addictions and reactive patterns into freedom and bliss.

While meditating we are not trying to conjure up a particular mood or recreate a past feeling, i.e. memory referencing, or thinking 'I must let go', or engaging in any kind of internal dialogue. The simple, exclusive use of the mantra innately induces calm, so that we are not thinking about anything or latching onto the nature of any thoughts that may arise, good or bad. This is our non-active time, which ultimately leads to the integration of the finite conscious mind with the illusory subconscious, which becomes consciousness – like raindrop merging with ocean, finite mind fusing with infinite mind.

This process develops 'knowing' through unknowing, a realm of 'you' being absent and God being present. It makes conscious the Kingdom of God, which resides within your spiritual heart; virgin-consciousness giving birth to your Christ child within.

You will not be alone on this journey, for 'Lo, I am with you even unto the ends of the world', meaning until the end of suffering. From this moment, refuse to live in the psychic sleep state, the subconscious conditioning, but instead 'lift up your heart' to the light. Claim your heavenly inheritance, your full humanity, the spirit of God. This one precious diamond is worth trading all your glass marbles for. This jewel is your entitlement, your God-given gift, let no one or no thing keep it from you, 'For it is His Will that you shall have the Kingdom, and have it in abundance'.

Spirit of Love

The Spirit moves within me now,
expression, seeking life.
God, I ask to be the heart
to give this loving truth away,
be a channel for your Spirit,
giving life to smiles and hugs,
laughter, goodwill, acceptance and forgiveness;
beauty, love creates.
God, I am thankful for this unending
source of love within.

The Spirit moves within me now,
wisdom, seeking birth.
God, I feel your message in my heart,
to bring your light to those still lost,
seek and praise a crying-out soul,
share this love with those in need.
See love in all,
treat all as love.
God, let this awareness felt within
grow to do your perfect will.

The Spirit moves within me now,
understanding, seeking words.
God, let thy words expressed through me,
unite and heal divided minds,
for loving hearts to multiply.
Speaking truth with trust and cleansed with love,
God, let my Spirit soar,
to city, town and nation,
to free your gift in all mankind.

Heaven in Earth

Trust in the Lord with all thine heart;
and lean not unto thine own understanding.
In all thy ways acknowledge him,
and he shall direct thy paths.

(Proverbs 3:5–6)

One of the most well-known, beloved and powerful prayers of the major religions is, indeed, *The Lord's Prayer*. Brilliantly crafted by the Master Himself, it is a series of positively worded affirmations stated in the present tense; an acknowledgement by Jesus of present-moment authentic awareness, divine-consciousness, our Father. When understood, both intellectually and experientially, then this is, indeed, the way we should pray. This was taught to the Apostles as a spiritual code to live by, who then went on to propagate this understanding, experiencing transformation of consciousness, hence the Gospels.

By praying or living the ethos of *The Lord's Prayer*, we are declaring divine order as our expression, as our manifestation supply source. It is how we should pray for our needs, both physical and spiritual, and for those of our neighbour. By repeating *The Lord's Prayer* with love and from spiritual understanding – raised consciousness – then, indeed, these words are powerful.

The following would be the general spiritual understanding of *The Lord's Prayer*:

'Our Father', meaning the father is the giver to the child. The child asks and expects to receive from the father. 'Which art in Heaven', God is always in heaven and heaven is always perfect. 'Hallowed be thy Name', holy, healing, loving, compassionate; 'hallowed be thy Nature'.

'Name' in the Bible symbolises the nature of someone or something. So, holy, healing, loving, compassionate, be God's name/nature. 'Thy Kingdom come', because we are feeling really well in ourselves in the presence of God, we acknowledge that moment as 'Thy Kingdom come'. 'Thy Will be done in Earth as it is in Heaven' – in the Bible, the word 'earth' refers to our physical body, our family and our business affairs, so by these words we're declaring that heaven, i.e. perfect health, happiness and prosperity, be present in all these areas.

'Give us this day our daily bread', meaning we're not to live solely from yesterday's happiness, success and contentment, but to come to the Father daily for it. 'Bread' in this case means soul nourishment. 'And forgive us our trespasses as we forgive those who trespass against us' – if we have transgressed the laws of God and seek to ask God for favours, yet may be holding back on forgiving some other person or situation, how can we expect the forgiveness or divine peace of mind that only God can provide? (Also, 'Before ye enter the temple, forgive', means before you enter the heart chamber within your consciousness, forgive.)

'And lead us not into temptation, but deliver us from evil' – as we evolve spiritually we become highly sensitive and, for example, someone's remark, intentionally or otherwise, can be deeply hurtful. So here we are asking that we are not tempted to be hurt by listening through our ego or that we are not tempted to keep thinking it over, but that we always possess sufficient spiritual understanding; 'evil' meaning that we don't fall back into ignorance; that we remain compassionate.

And God said, 'To one who overcomes I will give a white stone with a new name written on it'. The new name is our new nature, our new spiritual nature. At this stage we are living heaven in earth, from raised consciousness, our nature in divine harmony. Through our daily meditation our conditioned subconscious is integrated, thus leaving our heart and nervous system purified, while our conscious mind becomes expanded to experience the true nature of the divine – awakened-consciousness. As one Bible writer put it, we have turned our desert, our wilderness, into a bed of sweet-smelling roses. We have become transformed spiritually within our consciousness to live our lives according to divine purpose – to live God's nature of love, peace and contentment in abundance, knowing that The Father, through our meditation, prayer, is providing us with our daily bread, soul nourishment.

This transformation of consciousness through meditation, prayer, into spiritual understanding is our second birth, the birth which Jesus spoke of as 'Unless a man be born again of water and the Spirit he cannot enter into the Kingdom of God'. 'Born again' is the shedding of the subconscious conditioning to reveal our already present state of divine-consciousness. We are simply giving birth to our inner Christ-child through our awakened virgin-consciousness, which was always there but covered over by conditioning. Now, through our meditation, the winter is over and our new Christ-consciousness blossoms in full glory within our hearts; the second coming of Christ. The kingdom of God is surely at hand, now.

This is the process of redemption, of redeeming our spirit from the wilderness of the subconscious, conditioned mind and entering into unity-consciousness – cosmic-consciousness – when our mind becomes infused with the nature of bliss, Christ-consciousness, which cannot be known through a lower state. This is why daily meditation is vital; it provides the portal through which the state of bliss is achieved.

Remember, we don't create bliss, peace or happiness or try to give ourselves something. The bliss nature and all its attributes are already present within our consciousness. Just as the sun is already present behind the clouds, waiting for them to clear away, so is our inner bliss waiting for the gap in our thoughts to shine through in its magnificence. It is our meditation, our non-activeness, our non-effort of being mentally still through the use of the mantra that unlocks the bliss seal to release the divine state, the 'heaven in earth' state. When thinking of heaven, see this in terms of meaning happiness and peace of mind. And see earth as meaning perfect health within your physical being, state of consciousness and life situations. This is what we are each here to express.

Giving birth to heaven on earth, or heaven in earth, is a natural, effortless, automatic process. There is nothing extraordinary we need to do to achieve heaven; in fact, it is our non-doing while in meditation that is the catalyst to divinity. Meditation is the dynamic that allows the clouds to clear away to reveal our inner sun, the tombstone to roll back and reveal the risen Christ within. Once the nature of the Christ light is revealed to us experientially, it will never wane or dim. Once we have given birth to Christ-consciousness, for us then, it is 'heaven in earth'. We then live that state of divine bliss, thus ensuring that God's purpose is being fulfilled through us playing our vital part in His creation. Once enlightenment has been attained, we just carry on manifesting God's abundance into the world, in all its formats, to benefit and inspire others and to glorify the kingdom.

He Leads Us

Who knows our every need, who sent His word as creed,
who knows the peace we hunger for each day;
who sent His spirit bright, that we might see the light,
whose love is it each day that guides our way.

Who takes us out of night, renews us by His light,
whose love so glows to tell us we're His own;
who finds us when we're lost, whose light shines through
the dark,
who guides us when we're searching to come home.

Who made the oceans pound, filled hearts of love abound,
who gives to us the waves of joy we crave;
whose spirit never wanes, with us does it remain,
whose name proclaims that love should be our ways.

Who leads us to His peace, our spirit to release,
who leads us by His grace so patiently;
He is the one true Lord, His love brings such accord,
He leads each one to joy eternally.

Your Trophy

Each one of us has received a special gift
in proportion to what Christ has given.

(Ephesians 4:7)

In the City of Dublin where I grew up, I would often go for long walks
in preparation for the Dublin City Marathon. Frequently, while on these
walks, I would visit one of the many beautiful churches dotted around
the city and the outskirts to say a few prayers and to meditate. It always
amazed me that, with all the hustle and bustle of the traffic, and the
general noise of a thriving city such as Dublin, here was a sanctuary, a
refuge of peace and tranquillity, a place of heavenly and profound
silence, with maybe only two or three praying souls inside or sometimes
even empty.

Inside the church, one statue in particular fascinated me; the statue
with 'Emanuel' written on it, which means 'God with us'. This
particular statue is of a saint holding a child on one arm and glancing
upwards. The wonderful teaching portrayed here is that the saint is
holding up his inner Christ-child, raising to heaven his indwelling
Christ-consciousness for all to see, expressing his spiritual dimension
and sharing his light out into the world.

Occasionally, while at home or with friends, we might look at and
reminisce over old trophies that we picked up in competitions over the
years. We relive the special events as the memories come flooding back
to us; that great moment of the supreme effort that got us over the
winning line, scored that goal, jumped that height, achieved that target
or whatever it was that assured us of getting our hands on that trophy
and holding it up.

Here, in the church, we see the saint doing just that; holding up his trophy, not in any boastful or egotistical manner, but as light that others may see. He is carrying his trophy, his light, around in his heart, so that it can easily be seen, not only by a few family friends and well-wishers, like with our sideboard trophies, but by the whole world.

Sometimes, just wearing a smile, extending a warm handshake or simply being present to another with our awareness is holding up our trophy, our inner child, by allowing our inner peace to shine out like a healing beacon, so that others may be inspired and benefit from it; even those with whom we may not come into physical contact. This is serving the divine purpose here on earth; letting others see our trophy, our inner light, without any fuss or effort, but in a calm and relaxed manner. Let it be simple, natural and practical and let it be interpreted and expressed from our spiritual heart.

God has awarded each of us a trophy; that is, our heavenly trophy, our own indwelling Christ. There is no need to enter competitions or strenuous events such as a marathon to receive this. No, instead, we need only to accept, experience and express our trophy. Let it simply expand and reach out unconditionally, so that our essence may touch others.

We received this precious gift at birth. Have you unwrapped and experienced your gift yet? You can do this now, by learning to meditate. This will lift up your heart and raise your level of consciousness. Live the success, the happiness that your trophy represents. Live the full stature of your indwelling Christ, as in 'I come that you may have Life, and have it in abundance'.

Stand up on the podium of light now and accept your gift. It is yours, be glad, be happy, you have been given the kingdom. Yes, just like the saint, you, too, have been given the trophy of light. Release the vibrations of love and happiness that are the nature of your trophy. Hear the anthem of the spirit proclaim you as a true recipient, a merited receiver. Do your lap of honour, live your trophy, let it be seen. Shine your light from within, let your trophy be that which illuminates the world – a prism that reflects the light silently yet brilliantly.

Refuse to allow your trophy to grow dim. Keep it fuelled, keep it in use and love, peace and all that is the nature of God will be your expressive nature, too. Choose to use your trophy to lift the hearts of others. Remember, the 'cup' can fill up quickly and if this full cup is not expressed it becomes stagnant, non-creative energy. In order for new wisdom, understanding and love to be constantly flowing into your cup, you must empty or express that which you have received already – 'my cup runneth over'. It is in giving that we receive.

By learning the practice of meditation and through the continued expression of our new expanded awareness, we induce the raising of our consciousness, thus ensuring that the light of our trophy remains switched on, permanently. Meditation is life-supporting and soul-nourishing, bringing bliss to the heart and into our lives, becoming our daily state of mind, our way of life, our permanent state of consciousness. As we express love and goodwill, we enjoy the nature of love and well-being within our own physical body and environment. Simply by being in our true nature and by expressing the qualities of peace and harmony, we are actively helping and guiding others' paths to the same light, to the same blissful state of mind.

With each new trophy beaming its light, more and more souls are becoming inspired to be likewise, to be light bearers, to be trophy holders, thus contributing to the raising of the global vibrations of God-consciousness.

Peace

As I journey Lord my path with Thee
let me be a servant of Thy peace.
Emit to all a radiance bright,
touching hearts with heavenly light.
That all my deeds in cheerful mode
a peace create through peace bestowed.

And that I may this blessed day
Thy will fulfil in every way.
That all my giving nurtures living,
a joyful creed for those in need.
Freely share Thy treasure-gift
of priceless peace for to uplift.

And for this day through words I say
my every sound in harmony be.
Through every toil, a pause in smile,
to all I greet, Thy measure meet.
For as is light a joy to see
Thy heavenly beam to shine through me.

Communication

Let every soul be subject unto the higher powers.
For there is no power but of God:
the powers that be are ordained of God.

(Romans 13:1)

Let us say the mind is similar in effect to a transmitting station, constantly sending and receiving signals as thoughts of ourselves and others. Let us say, for instance, that we are transmitting unhappy, angry, negative thoughts. Then it is that nature of these thoughts or signals that we attract back to us. The mind, as we said, acting like a transmitter, can also receive the nature of other people's angry moods and negativity, if that is what it is tuned in to. Likewise, if we're sending out vibrations of goodwill, peace and love, then this is the nature of our incoming vibrations – like attracts like. When spiritually awakened, there is added responsibility to always watch the newly heightened sensitivity of our 'receiving station', as we are easily repulsed and emotionally upset by conflict or by any type of negativity.

'Jesus and the Apostles got into the Boat and went to the other side of the lake'. When we set out to meet family, friends, neighbours and so on, we try to greet them with a smile and a warm handshake to make the encounter as pleasant and as uplifting as possible. So it was with the Apostles: they were spiritually awakened individuals going on their mission, their vocation, to greet the other side of life – the state of ignorance – on their way to uplift those in need of spiritual help. The boat was their individual states of Christ-consciousness, which is a peaceful, loving, calm state of heart and mind, and they were 'transmitting' those good vibrations and would receive the same in return: 'As ye sow, so shall ye reap'.

The Apostles went out to sow the seed, hoping for the harvest of healing and leading others back to the way – to the path, to the nature of God. They were going out to preach on the other side of the lake, meaning the other side of life, which is the state of ignorance and all that entails, such as stress, phobias, fears and depression – suffering. The Apostles, through Christ-consciousness, had the answer within their hearts and minds to all the negativity of their day and they were going to share their manna – soul-nourishment – with anyone who would listen.

The practice of meditation leads one to Christ-consciousness. When a person has gained this state, when greeting and communicating with others, they are actually greeting the Christ of the other person, even if that person has not attained the same state of awareness. We love the spirit of the other as our own, as in 'Love thy neighbour as thy Self'.

Of course, we deplore their wrong actions or inappropriate words, but as self-realised spiritual beings we recognise that compassion is in the nature of Christ-consciousness. By demonstrating compassion we are expressing the will of God, acknowledging divine unity with the unrealised spirit of the other, thereby understanding – 'Forgive them Father for they know not what they do'.

They are living from the state of ignorance which, in modern terms, is called subconscious programming or conditioning. God is communicating with each of us on a moment-to-moment basis, but it is this impure state of consciousness that distorts this divine communication. This state will continue until the person eliminates it through meditation or some other mind-expansion programme. This process gives birth to self-realisation, which is God to the rescue; hence, 'And He descended into hell', meaning that God, love, bliss, descends into the suffering and eradicates it.

The level of our freed consciousness, our reclaimed awareness, determines the level of bliss that we experience – 'In my Father's Kingdom there are many mansions', symbolising that there are many levels of consciousness, higher states of awareness, in the kingdom for us to come into. Put another way, whatever colour tints the glasses that we're looking through, will be the shade of our life experiences and the nature of our communication. Purity of heart and mind, through the daily discipline of meditation, is the secret of expanded awareness – higher states of consciousness.

'If there be only one just man I will save the city' – symbolises that the person in meditation is the one just man or woman and Christ will save them from the suffering of the world – their thoughts, worries and fears – and He will set their consciousness in harmony with truth, which is inner freedom. This quote clearly describes the invitation to enlightenment, the acceptance of which is a personal venture within one's own consciousness, leading to self-discovery – bliss-consciousness.

Once having commenced this inner journey to enlightenment, be assured that you will not find Christ lacking in His presence – 'Lo, I am with you even unto the ends of the world'. Your indwelling Christ-consciousness will be present to dissolve your stress, fears and anxiety – the state of ignorance – hell. You are that one just man or woman that Christ is waiting to save, to cleanse and to purify, so that you may enjoy and reflect the kingdom, His nature. He awaits within the silent chamber of your heart for you to still your reasoning, analytical mind, to communicate with you through the use of the mantra in meditation.

This is the great transformation, the great alchemy of our spirit: darkness into light, water into wine, suffering to bliss, the birth of the Eternal spirit in us – the born-again-of-the-spirit state, which Jesus referred to so many times.

Our daily practice of meditation brings us to enlightenment. This is the opportunity to surrender our falseness to the miraculous healing power of God, to then live life in abundance through pure communication from His authentic wisdom.

In the Bible, Lazarus was raised to spiritual life, raised in Christ-consciousness to live in freedom from the bondage of ignorance, sin. When we meditate we, too, are raised in consciousness, awakened in heart to communicate spiritually through our fully-developed consciousness-awareness capacity. We've arrived in the 'Promised Land'.

Our inner lamp, our heart and mind, is fuelled with the purest oil and we can see our path clearly now. We are connected to our source – God, love, wisdom and understanding. We cannot possibly run out of this oil and become lost, as the biblical sister did; she slipped out of present-moment awareness and became careless with her thoughts – she had lost the conscious contact of pure communication. Through her state of ignorance, of being spiritually unaware, she entertained thoughts of worry, fear and negativity, the cost of which is to be lost in suffering.

Through regular meditation our ordinary human consciousness becomes the raised state of awareness which, in effect, becomes our 'oil', our source. Our Eternal spiritual flame thus guides our every thought and action in life, hence the line of *The Lord's Prayer*, 'Thy Will be done in earth as it is in Heaven'. This line becomes our daily reality as we communicate, express and manifest peace, love and happiness from divine wisdom.

Our spiritual awakening influences whoever we communicate with. Even the environment begins to resonate with love and peace – we can see and feel the unity and goodness that underlies all of creation; in people, animals and the natural world. Through meditation we develop resolute intellect in the form of depth and clarity of thought, mental focus, inner poise, a balanced approach, a sense of harmony and compassion. We become less reactionary, we remain calm in turbulent situations and we don't get overexcited in pleasant ones!

Listening is said to be the art of good communication and because sharing our manna, our understanding, requires of us to be good listeners, we practice meditation to help us become more centred, more deeply in present-moment awareness. This allows us to be more generous of spirit, more tolerant and fulsome in our attention to others – listening from the heart. Thus, we can relate to the biblical words 'He healed the deaf and the blind' as meaning He healed their hearts, so that they could then hear and see from spiritual awareness.

'I go before thee' – as awakened spiritual beings, God-consciousness now fills our hearts and all of our actions stem from that divine state of awareness: 'The Kingdom of Heaven'. By sharing our manna, our spiritual love and understanding, by communication through our inner Sacred Heart, Christ-consciousness, we are each of us, as the Apostles, no matter what denomination, creed or colour, furthering the creator's plan.

Wonders

The freedom o'er a meadow
and fields in summer sway,
the language of the oceans
and all the waves at play;
The rustle of high trees,
the splendour of a dawn,
the wind in tuneful bellow,
the wonder e'er I'm drawn.

The calm o'er rugged mountains,
the sound among the hills,
the silence of the universe
and all the space it fills;
The magic of warm sunshine,
of hearts that bloom divine,
the seed, the shower, the heavenly flower,
the wonder e'er so fine.

To pause in awe, the winter thaw
and colour come sweet spring,
a season's way to brighter day,
the promise nature brings;
To while in, oh, a river's flow
and trickles clear, so dear,
the simple tones o'er pebble stones,
the wonder e'er so near.

To sit engrossed, as nature hosts
these wonders all around,
that I should hear with heart sincere
creation in unbound;
And I to give, my life to live
the journey, as a cloud,
that His great will, my joy to fill
the wonder e'er I'm vowed.

Lose Yourself to Find Yourself

Do not lie to one another,
for you have taken off the old self
with its habits
and have put on the new self.

(Colossians 3:9–10)

For many years, I must confess, while still in my state of ignorance, this one line of wisdom used to baffle me. After all, when no one has educated us of its understanding and meaning, and of how we can possibly go about losing ourself in order to find ourself, it is difficult to grasp. Of course, when one becomes enlightened of its meaning, one has by then automatically 'lost your self' and truly 'found your self!' But, I can assure the reader that there was a time when I didn't know how to go about this process and the cost of such ignorance, sadly to say, was suffering. I've been there.

So now, happily, we will shed some light on this line. The self whom we lose is the ego-created 'small' self, which exists in the illusion of its own finite self-importance. It is an illusion, because in essence it isn't real; it is just the collection of conditioning that has been impressed upon our psyche: mind, heart, and nervous system. The end product of such 'small' self-conditioning is the subconscious mind, the state of ignorance, the state of perpetual suffering or, in religious terms, the state of sin or darkness.

The small self is like a high-powered mental chatterbox, which never ceases, until we go to sleep maybe if it lets us, but as soon as we wake up it is off again. It is always trying to deal with some imaginary loss, trying out of fear to get ahead and striving for more as if that is where ultimate happiness will be found on some distant day. The small self is always restless, anxious, worrying, and it feeds on these conditions. States like stillness, peace, love and contentment are difficult for it to entertain.

Now we will consider the self we want to find. This capital 'S' self, which is our Eternal Christ nature, requires the process of mind expansion in order for it to be revealed. Meditation naturally dissolves the stress and anxiety that is maintaining the small self, leading to mind expansion which, with regular practice, will bring into our experiential nature bliss-consciousness, which is our true self. Thus, we lose our small self and find our higher spiritual self, our inner Christ-child consciousness – 'for unto us a Child is born'. So now we can see how the small self is the imposed, conditioned persona; it is an impostor who masks our true self from shining through our being.

Losing the small self is really losing the conditioned subconscious. Although most people appear to be living normal lives they are, in fact, to some degree, living out subconscious reactive patterns over which they have no control. This is how high-powered advertising works, too: the senses are manipulated by a message planted in the mind. This message, whenever triggered, is reactivated automatically over and over in the subconscious, so that we keep doing, or buying, whatever it was.

Similarly, we are conditioned by society, country, family or peers and through ignorance, we accept this state of living as normal and then wonder why we are unhappy and addicted to things. Through this ignorance many live in hardship and misery, which could easily be prevented by education in this area but, nevertheless, it is each person's own responsibility to 'first seek The Kingdom'.

So how then do we break free from subconscious reactive patterns and lose the small self? While this at first may seem complicated, it is really very simple: we learn the art of meditation. In doing so, the addictive nature of the small self will be dissipated and integrated into our higher self and through sustained and regular practice we find our bliss, our true self, and we live in spiritual freedom for the first time ever. Now we understand the wonderful biblical saying 'The Truth shall set you free'. The truth is our higher self, our inner Christ-consciousness, and this sets us free from the bondage of the suffering caused by subconscious conditioning.

When Moses, in the Bible, led his people into the Promised Land, it was to this higher state of consciousness that he was leading them. By losing the small self we are shedding the state of ignorance, darkness, and we are reclaiming the Promised Land, the state of spiritual consciousness within.

Also, in the Bible story of David, the shepherd boy who slew Goliath the giant, David had the white marble, i.e. the light, Christ-consciousness, in his breast pocket, i.e. in his heart. Goliath, the giant, represents the seemingly overwhelming state of ignorance, of darkness and misery, but David – the light – overcame Goliath – the darkness: the higher self overcame the small self. By learning to meditate we can do the same: 'lose your self to find your Self'.

Heaven Sent Me You

How many waves make up the sea,
or raindrops in a shower,
how many storms can rage upon
the petals of a flower;
How many dreams can fade away,
melt with the morning dew,
oh, how things changed
when heaven sent me You.

How many stones make up the road
are heartaches to be known,
how many tears can one heart cry
before the way is shown;
How many times can time repeat
old lessons dressed as new,
oh, how things changed
when heaven sent me You.

How many stars make up the sky,
or moonbeams in a night,
and what is distance to the road
when there is so much light;
How much sunshine fills the sun,
it's summer all year through,
oh, how things changed
when heaven sent me You.

I've known so many hurts before
but Your love is so real,
a soothing humming in my heart,
how good it makes me feel;
Oh, love is in my life once more,
a miracle it's true,
oh, how things changed
when heaven sent me You.

Intuition

and you must put on the new self,
which is created in God's likeness
and reveals itself in the true life
that is upright and holy.

(Ephesians 4:24)

When we first take up the practice of meditation or any mind-expansion programme, a peeling away of the layers of the old, conditioned state begins to occur: coatings of soul toxins are removed, just like dust from a mirror, in order to reveal our true nature, which has been covered over for so long: 'They wandered in the desert for forty years'. We notice new insights emerging, 'one-liners' of wisdom, of intuition, as our newborn divine-consciousness expands. This is also referred to as integration of the heart and mind, the healing of our separation from God. Intuition means tuition from within, hence in-tuition; authentic wisdom of the Spirit, authentic wisdom of God.

Most people are living at some level of gross surface awareness, rarely becoming still enough mentally to experience the more refined, subtle states of spiritual awareness or resolute intellect. Hence, 'intuition' remains for them the prompting of the ego self, where authorship of wisdom and manifestations is credited to the conditioned mind, which is the conscious mind thinking by itself.

By contrast, through meditation, authentic intuition bypasses the conscious mind, whereby the individual mind becomes universal consciousness, finite mind becoming infinite mind. This is when all our thoughts, at our conscious point of use, are that of authentic wisdom, intuitiveness, pure awareness. Intuitive knowledge, as opposed to rational knowledge, pervades our consciousness as understanding such that new spiritual perceptions flood our awareness. Finally, we acknowledge the silent voice within, intuition, which is the Holy Spirit, meaning the holistic Spirit, or Spirit of wholeness. This marks the beginning of self-realisation. If we remain always at the level of surface awareness, it is difficult for us to recognise, trust or appreciate authentic intuitive knowledge. For this reason we need to still the analysing, egotistical mind, transcend the rational thinking mind, become absorbed in mental silence and just 'be', as in human 'be ing'.

Without meditation we are always going to be operating from the conditioned subconscious state and thereby our so-called wisdom, our judgements, can be considered as 'flawed'. We cannot be sure, or trust, that our decisions fall into the category of 'Thy Will be done'. It is more a case of 'my will be done'.

With meditation, on the other hand, through regular and sustained practice, we can become one with source, authentic wisdom, and thence can trust our decisions as being in accordance with the laws of God, natural law, with the natural flow of the evolutionary process. Our hearts and minds are no longer jammed in between radio stations, getting mixed signals, but are tuned instead to authentic knowledge. Our purpose then conforms to God's Will.

Clarity of thought prevails: a sense of knowingness, of truth, permeates our inner being, our consciousness. No longer are we fearful, no longer do we feel threatened or isolated, but rather we remain feeling calm, happy and confident; in control and not out of control. With intuition we don't have to remember so much detail, for we are 're-membered' and fulfilled from within throughout all phases of our life. It is a case of 'Bull's Eye' from wherever we may pitch our resolute intellect. Intuitive knowledge brings about enlightened understanding. Intuition is then acknowledged as the wisdom of God and we are the consciousness expressing the divine principle – divine revelation being played out through us, the instruments, and divine law, the conductor.

Divine will requires that the channel through which His wisdom flows is sufficiently spiritually purified so as to reflect, with clarity, the divine understanding, the divine intention: 'Thy Will be done'. This is why meditation ought to be a twice-daily routine, for this is the surest way to right action in our lives and for God's plan to unfold. It leads us to pure-consciousness, pure awareness, which is the criterion of right action, as this can only be determined by the degree of purity of our level of consciousness. Right action is always life-supporting, evolutionary, always in harmony with natural law, the divine will. Right action is the outcome of conscious intuition of the divine and meditation brings about this pure state of consciousness into our minds, physiology, nervous system and senses. This is why we should afterwards engage in our normal activities, thus ensuring infusion of heavenly consciousness, permanently – our life eternally flowing in harmony and balance from divine intuition.

Tree of Life

Relaxed within the centred space,
seeking source of nourished root,
easing back the hurried stride,
nature's pace providing growth.

Sweetness, clearness, gaining strength,
expanding beauty by expression,
humour, goodwill, friendliness,
attracting dwellers to my branch.

Happy leaves performing duty,
breathing out the breath of life,
swaying gracefully with the wind,
relaxed in root's connected source.

Silent moments with creator,
sustaining wisdom for my growth,
nourished seed reveals its glory,
towering tree, divine in purpose.

Saving God

'But God, who is rich in mercy,
for his great Love wherewith He loved us,
even when we were dead in sins,
hath quickened us together with Christ,
(by grace ye are saved;)'

(Ephesians 2:4–5)

The natural intuitive desire of every person is for God to save them. From day one this is absolutely our perfect prayer, for not only will God save us, but He already has saved us, whether we realise it, or silently or verbally express it, or not. The moment we make it known to the kingdom that we want 'saving', we are making it 'official', maybe after life has been prompting us with some hardship or miseries of sorts. This request is fulfilling the biblical saying 'first seek the Kingdom'. When life becomes so unbearable, it is time to acknowledge the suffering, get off the misery-go-round of ignorance and raise the white flag: surrender resistance to life. This white flag signifies victory, not defeat; victory to our awareness, of hearing God's prompt from within.

So our first job is to seek the kingdom, the nature of which is love and peace, and heavenly bliss, and to proclaim that nature, through our existence, identify and become that nature within our consciousness, and to express this new spiritually-raised awareness in our daily activities. When the Bible uses the word 'Name', it means the 'nature' of the thing, which in this case, because it is spelled with a capital 'N', means the nature of God or Christ-consciousness. Therefore, when we say 'in My Name' or 'in God's Name', we're actually saying 'in God's nature'.

Let us look more closely at other phrases we may use; like 'God, please save me'. When we utter sentiments like this we are really asking for God to save the small egotistical 'me' – the unrealised state. We mean save me, yes, but leave everything else as it is; sins, ego and all!

But the kingdom doesn't work like that, because first we are going to have to shed some baggage. Setting out to seek God is not like journeying abroad for a holiday with loads of suitcases, but quite the opposite, for the very things that we're trying to hold on to internally are the very things that are going to be let go, through integration and healing. Those very things are what caused our suffering in the first place: our conditioned, programmed behaviour, stored in the baggage compartment of our subconscious mind. We cannot bring the darkness of our baggage into the light, but God will bring His light into that darkness, as in 'And He descended into hell'. That darkness, hell, is the subconscious state of ignorance; our ignorance of truth, of light.

Then, through integration of our baggage, God becomes our conscious presence, through experiential awareness. His nature being transcendental, it lies the other side of our subconsciousness, the other side of our relative nature – our unconscious psychic sleep state of heart and mind. This unconscious state needs bringing back to life, just as Lazarus was. It needs to be raised, 'saved', reclaimed and brought into consciousness. Losing this unconscious, unrealised state is what is going to save us and save us now while on this earthly plane, not at some imaginary time in the future.

God is now a living reality for us, a real inner presence that fills both the mind and heart with bliss, so that our 'cup runneth over' with wisdom, peace and understanding. We have moved away from the mere intellectualising of God, to the experiential level.

Jesus said 'If you love Me keep My Commandments'. Love in this case is not an emotional love, it is a way of life, an unconditional well-being of spirit, the already present presence of the 'Me', in you; which is the indwelling Christ, the real you within. And love being God's nature, this has to be expressed through you, your spirit, in order for you to experience it. 'No-one can get to the Father except through Me'.

By embarking on a meditation programme we are setting out to save God, which already exists within us, but which we must bring to the conscious level of our awareness. Our intention of saving God within us actually turns into God saving us! By seeking God as our nature, we find our self saved and in His kingdom, in our raised state of God-consciousness. We gain salvation, redemption, bliss-consciousness and the direct experience of saved God, saved self, the real you, the only you which the kingdom recognises.

It was the baggage of past ignorance, worries and fears, or the conditioned state, that was the cause of our miseries. The hiding of our self from God was, in fact, our automatic subconscious ignorance, but it was all we could do at the time – 'Forgive them Father, for they know not what they do'.

Somewhere along the way, through all our distress, through all our turmoil, fears and anxieties, we called out in despair, something along the lines of 'I've had enough of this; there must be more to life than all this wretchedness' – 'Why hast thou forsaken Me?' At this point our cry, our prayer, became intentional, as we sought a spiritual solution to a worldly condition, to eliminate the gap between ignorance and enlightenment, between suffering and bliss. We raised the white flag. All that was needed was to signal to the other side our intention to surrender and when the pupil is ready the Master is willing.

Our meditation sessions are our surrender times. We become detached from our 'problems' and the transformation, the healing, the rejuvenation and the expansion of our consciousness then takes place, bringing God into our awareness. Here, He is realised and experienced as love, bliss, heaven, becoming a living reality within our being, within our heart and mind. Thus, is our meditation 'saving God'.

What Reason

If each of us could be, at peace within we'd see
that we are all reflectors of His love.
For love is what we are; a light just like a star,
and it's waiting for to beam out in the world.

Let us give, oh let us try, let us fill the world with joy,
let us share the peace and brightness of our love.
Let us reach out, let us begin, let us free the light within,
for love's the only reason why we should.

What radiance can we beam, what sunshine can be seen,
what light can there be if there is no love.
What vision be so bright, or wondrous the sight,
what loving heart does not reflect the sun.

What magic can be drawn, from what we gaze upon,
what beauty fills the heart if love is gone.
What measure be our aim, what pleasure be our gain,
what treasure be so rich if there's no love.

Let us rise above the mire, let us shine, let us aspire,
let us show the world a light that all can see.
What reason do we need, to let our love be seen,
what reason do we need to set love free.

The Peace that Passeth ...

And the peace of God,
which passeth all understanding,
shall keep your hearts and minds
through Christ Jesus.

(Philippians 4:7)

This wonderful expression, 'The Peace that passeth all understanding', contains the promise that awaits those who seek to follow the path of enlightenment, who seek to participate in the most glorious of journeys that one can ever embark upon. It is the journey of alpha and omega, which simply means the journey through the beginning of the end of suffering. It is the journey to our inner self, of self-discovery, bringing an end to the greatest sin of all life; the ignorance of our true nature, which is bliss-consciousness.

As we progress in life we come upon great readings and insights by people who have successfully trodden this most precious and personal of journeys. Their insights in regards to spiritual progress and self-realisation are like outer markers that we identify with, relate to and take heart from, as they influence our direction. They fill us with assurance, reminders and awareness, making us feel confident that we are doing the right thing. Each inspirational saying uplifts us with a degree of understanding, which can help us in some big or small way on our journey. Remember, it is the journey which is the goal and the great readings and insights, while invaluable as they are for their wisdom and courage-building, are in no way a substitute for the experience of the journey itself.

The journey is all about our journeying to God. It is a process of unknowing, of deconditioning, of deepening our experiential contact with the Almighty. God is presence, presence is heaven, heaven is pure existence. God requires no understanding of in order for us to experience 'The Peace that passeth all understanding', but, however it is first necessary for us each to embark upon the journey of subconscious mind purification. As the process continues we then 'become' that peace, with no understanding of it required to attain it. Quite the opposite, in fact, because God is beyond human comprehension.

During meditation we drop all that we think we know; our opinions, our understanding, including all the great words of wisdom we may have read or heard; all our intellectualising and memory referencing to past or future ceases. With daily practice, meditation automatically brings us to that peace, to that bliss that passeth all understanding. It is like the metal and the magnet; at a certain point, they are both irresistibly drawn to each other, until contact is achieved. The goal, the permanent conscious contact with that transcendent peace, is achieved by direct experiencing on a daily basis. Readings satisfy the mind, but meditation fulfils the heart. Yes, readings can provide the mind with some relative peace and basic intellectual understanding is desirable, but the heart needs the direct experience of love, of bliss. We need reliable and relatable information on spiritual matters to give us a footing and mental guidance on the subject, but a signpost only points in the direction, it does not provide the experience of the destination. Likewise, it is essential for us at certain times to put down our books and maps and enter into the destination. See and experience for ourselves at first-hand just what it is the saints and sages, Bible writers and other voices of enlightenment, of wisdom, are describing and why we need to get there. Instead of only reading the menu, we need to taste and eat the meal.

This, we achieve by entering into meditation, which is authentic prayer, the truth that sets us free. Jesus said 'Enter ye at the narrow gate'. This is the narrow gate through which we are entering – our own stilled, conscious mind. Simply sitting down in a chair and closing our eyes and engaging in meditation is like reaching out for the handle to that narrow gate and turning it to enter, where no one else can enter with us or for us. To boldly go where we have never gone before, which is to infinity and back, returning in a state of transformed consciousness, rolling back the tombstone of ignorance and resurrecting the Christ within. This journey takes us into the Eternal present moment, from self to Self, and once upon this path the prison shackles of the conditioned patterns of the subconscious mind are released.

We are following in the footsteps of the revered Bible explorers and saints and sages of all denominations, whose journeys before us provide us with the insights, the information and, most importantly, the techniques, to assist us in practising authentic prayer; prayer which makes actual conscious contact with the divine presence – God. We are, for sure, in gratitude to these peace seers. It is by that peace and into that 'Peace that passeth all understanding' that we enter while in meditation.

As our nervous system and physiology becomes more purified, a kind of subconscious detoxification comes about and our contact, our connection, with the Almighty becomes more and more deep, more blissful. Our capacity to withstand bliss, the heavenly state, increases to newer and higher levels of consciousness. To develop our capacity to experience this we are required, after meditation, to resume normal physical activities. It is very important that we don't sit around all day thinking about our wonderful new blissful experiences, that we do not retreat into a kind of monkish existence, but rather that we live and work in the marketplace and engage in our everyday affairs in a natural, easy way from our new evolving consciousness, our lives becoming more meaningful and fruitful as we do so.

This activity after meditation ensures the permanent infusion of bliss-consciousness into our hearts and minds, allowing our nervous system and physiology to reorientate and acclimatise. Through this expression of our purified living and actions, the journey, indeed, becomes the goal. As we express more and more the nature of 'the Peace' we become that nature. Gradually, our consciousness becomes transformed into His nature and we abide in Him, His peace. 'The Peace that passeth all understanding' is now a living reality for us.

Nature Affair

There's no place that I know, that's more peaceful to go,
than the place where true quietness abounds,
there to be at a glance, in a nature-romance,
and to dance with the sounds all around;

Hear the lakes and the crakes, see the dawn as it breaks,
feel the oneness of all this within,
to cherish, enfold, to praise and behold
all of nature's most wondrous things.

Where the spirit is pleased, to be calm and at ease,
for each moment is peace-sychronised,
to smell the sweet breeze, to embrace the tall trees,
or touch rivers that flow harmonised.

Then a trek in the woods, oh this feeling's so good;
just hear the soul's whispers within,
to cherish, enfold, to praise and behold
all of nature's most wondrous things.

Where the silence is pure, in a timeless measure,
yes, it's here we could grow, you and me,
for each moment spent there, in the nature affair,
gives a peace that is heaven surely.

Rich Man – Poor Man

Jesus answered, Verily, verily, I say unto thee,
Except a man be born of water and of the Spirit,
he cannot enter into the kingdom of God.

(St John 3:5)

Many of us may be familiar with the biblical saying 'It is as hard for a rich man to enter the kingdom of Heaven as for a camel to enter the eye of a needle'. Who, then, you may ask, is this 'rich man' (or 'rich woman'?)

Well, it is not the financially rich, the well-offs, the millionaires, those who may outwardly appear to have it all. The 'rich' in the quote are those who are caught up with their own self-importance, with lofty opinions of themselves, tending to lead with their over-inflated egos, caring little, or knowing little, of the qualities of the heart, of the spirit. Love, to them, in the spiritual sense, is not a priority, is difficult to relate to; indeed, it doesn't even enter the equation. Doing everything from a non-cosmically evolved state of consciousness, 'they' are always right – authorship of decisions is credited to their ego, to their 'me', the 'mine'. These 'rich' function from a conditioned personality, from their subconscious mind, from the state of spiritual ignorance. They are 'ego-rich'.

We should all ask regularly of ourselves, 'have I been acting the "camel" lately; have I been trying to get through the eye of the needle?' – am I 'ego-rich?' Through our ignorance of reality – our stressed-out state from our deadline-demanding, fast-food, fast-lane lifestyle – we could easily be 'richer' than we think. Our present state of mind, body and spirit, our well-being, our physical and mental health and whatever level of so-called happiness we may now be experiencing through our life situations is the barometer that indicates our 'rich' status.

Now let us consider another biblical saying: 'The poor shall inherit the earth'. This seems to be the complete opposite of the 'rich' individual we have just referred to and, in fact, that is what it is; the opposite, the other side of spiritual ignorance. The 'poor' are those who have shed the 'rich' (ego-rich) condition through meditation or other mind expansion work and they have become self-realised. The 'earth' which they inherit is the state of bliss within their consciousness, within their body, mind, heart, life situations, family and business. They, through their poverty of ego, inherit the kingdom.

In meditation we bring nothing with us; no possessions, opinions or egos – we become 'poor' without them. In meditation we have no personal agenda, no likes and dislikes, no trying to square the circle or squeeze some goodies out of God. The first principle of meditation is complete and utter surrender, with no internal dialogue or mental chatter and no plea bargaining for some desired outcome. We are relinquishing everything; our requests for this or that, our lists of demands and all that is of this world. The only thing that enters into meditation is inner silence through our mantra and it is through this state of 'poverty' that we access our inheritance, our bliss, and the quality of life which follows, as in 'First seek the Kingdom and all else shall be added'.

The mantra is really a sound which vibrates silently at the quantum level within our consciousness, our heart. It stirs the deeper levels of our being, our awareness. It is like diving into the ocean, finding the jewel on the ocean-bed, retrieving it and then bringing it to the surface for all to see. This jewel is more valuable than all the cash contained in bank vaults in the world. No amount of money, opinions or personality can purchase it. In fact, the transaction currency for it is inner mental stillness, poverty of ego and poverty of the conditioned state of ignorance, which is, of course, by way of contrast, in the spiritual sense, the 'rich' individual state.

The approach to becoming 'poor' is to 'raise the white flag' and the exchange, the response, will be love. Of course, we are not saying to physically give up material possessions, credit cards and the like, but we mean, for the duration of meditation, to come into the surrendered state of mind, the 'poor' individual state.

So, now, who is this rich man or woman? Paradoxically, through our meditation, our poverty of ego has led us to our true wealth – our heavenly state – the kingdom. We have, indeed, evolved from 'rich man' (or woman) to 'poor man' (or woman) which, in actuality, is from hell to heaven, from suffering to bliss.

When There Is You and Me

There's only warmth comes from the sun
and light from stars above,
there's only peace comes from a smile,
a beam of glowing love,
there's only treasure in my heart,
a splendour, oh, so free,
there's only moments so divine,
when there is You and me.

There's always roses reaching out,
with scented petals bright,
there's always dawns to gaze upon,
to bathe the heart in light,
there's always wings will soar on high
and lift so powerfully,
there's always love that fills the air,
when there is You and me.

There's always hours will slip away,
'goodnight my dearest friend',
for always love it lingers on,
'cause love it knows no end,
for always in my heart it feels
what seems eternity,
there's always bliss, which just persists,
when there is You and me.

Oh, Your presence it so elevates
the essence of my world,
You radiate a light to me
that wonders never could.
You'll always be that part of me
no beauty can compare,
for Your love I know eternally
will always be right there.

Watch With Me

And be not conformed to this world:
but be ye transformed by the renewing of your mind,
that ye may prove what is that good,
and acceptable, and perfect, will of God.

(Romans 12:2)

There are so many wonderful and life-changing sayings in the Bible and throughout scripture; great wisdom penned by earlier generations so long ago. These wise words act as spiritual signposts for the seeker of truth and reality. These saints and scholars were just ordinary folk like us, except that they were divinely inspired to seek the kingdom and to take whatever action was needed to achieve the spiritual awareness needed to bring about a transformation in their state of consciousness.

'Repent, Salvation is at hand'. The word 'repent' simply means to change our ways, to change our consciousness, to become transformed of heart and mind.

Of course, merely reading great wisdom in itself will not bring about transformation. While it can be spiritually uplifting, we still need to enter into deep mental silence, away from our thoughts, ego and personality. Remember, Jesus warned about aimlessly repeating words that carry no spiritual conviction.

'If you love Me keep My Commandments' means that we need a complete turnabout in our way of living if it is to be in harmony with the nature of God, for we cannot be saying that we love God in words, while at the same time be living from a lower subconscious level. We must raise our level to that of divine-consciousness, so that, like the saints, we are living in a devotional state of awareness, while carrying on with our normal daily activities.

'Do not take the Lord's Name in vain' means do not live 'in the name of God' that which is not the nature of God: the nature of God is love, contentment, peace of mind, health, prosperity and joyful abundance, so our lifestyles should be congruent with all of these spiritual values, for the good of ourselves and others, for the expansion of His kingdom. Like the saints, we are each called to divinity, to sainthood. In the Bible, when the Master sent out the servants to invite everyone to the wedding feast, the Kingdom, these servants are in fact the words of wisdom that we read in scriptures or that we hear from contemporary, self-realised people, inviting us into the kingdom. But first we must undergo a purification process of heart and mind and we must approach the kingdom through transformed consciousness.

When Jesus said 'Could you not watch one hour with Me?' He meant could the Apostles not stay awake within, stay awake in Christ-consciousness, in present-moment awareness, in the 'Me' of their own inner consciousness. In other words, watch their thoughts and not fall asleep spiritually, because wrong thinking would contaminate the state of their hearts and minds. This quote means that we are to spend some time every day away from this typical compulsive, repetitive thinking and instead to be 'watching with Me', 'watching' with our indwelling Christ – the transformational present moment within our being. (This 'Me' is spelt with a capital 'M' to denote Godhood, the infinite Eternal Christ self, whereas the small 'me' is the ordinary finite ego, the conditioned personality.) There are twenty-four hours in the day, so one hour isn't much to ask to 'watch with Me!' Nowadays, twenty minutes to half an hour spent meditating, i.e. 'watching', is generally recommended.

'No-one can get to the Father except through Me' means that we have to come into conscious contact with our indwelling 'Me', Christ – 'watch with Me' in order to enter the kingdom and 'get to the Father'. We are then 'repenting' or becoming transformed in heart and mind through spiritual awareness.

'I am the Lord thy God, thou shalt not have strange gods before Me' is the First Commandment, declaring that the Lord, the Law, God, is our here and now – 'I Am' consciousness. Anything opposed to His natural law, which comprises love, contentment, peace of mind, health, prosperity and joyful abundance, would be considered strange gods. Anything that does not resonate as His nature, such as anger, hatred, fear, worry, anxiety, all types of addictions and the illusory states of past and future would qualify as strange gods. We are meant to live according to His natural law, which we do by raising our ordinary human-consciousness, which is a conditioned state, to divine-consciousness, which is a purified state.

Adam, in the Bible, symbolises the first subconscious mind formed when he hid himself from God, from present-moment awareness, and decided to do things through his state of ignorance, instead of in harmony with natural law. And today, when we hide ourselves from the nature of God, by being angry or fearful or following our addictions, i.e. worshipping strange gods, we are not honouring the First Commandment. The subconscious conditioned mind comes into being while we are thus hiding from God's nature, the present moment; while we are out of our true divine nature, which then needs integration.

'When the Master was away the thieves entered' symbolises how the Master is our indwelling Christ-consciousness, our inner present-moment awareness, and the thieves are our wrong thoughts, negativity and conditioning, which in biblical terms is mortal sin; soul-destroying thinking. It is this type of mental activity which robs us of our well-being, because we're not in our present-moment awareness. The nature of our thoughts determines the nature of our mind; the quality of our mind reflects the nature of our thoughts, thus wrong-thinking – mortal sin – retards spiritual growth. The wise person leaves the light of their inner Christ-consciousness always switched on, so that the 'thieves' cannot rob them in the darkness of wrong-thinking. The thieves cannot operate in the presence of this light of God. God-realisation is an ongoing process, an every-day, every-moment vigilance of being constantly aware of the light switch and keeping it switched on permanently. It is what being 'present within' really means and like anything that is worthwhile, it needs mastering through regular practice.

One of the easiest ways to 'watch with Me' is the practice of meditation. This fulfils all of what Jesus is asking of us. It leads the mind gently and naturally into present-moment awareness, Christ-consciousness. It transforms and raises our ordinary consciousness, as Lazarus in the Bible was 'raised from the dead' – raised from mortal thinking. We see and hear from new levels of awareness and we understand what is meant when Jesus healed the blind and deaf: He healed their hearts, their consciousness, to see and to hear from the spiritual perception. When Jesus said 'I go before thee' he meant that our Christ-consciousness is already present in whatever actions we are performing: He is ever present as love in our hearts, our awareness and our intentions. Meditation unifies our hearts, minds and intentions, bringing us to a state of divine-consciousness – 'I and the Father are one.' The 'I' in these quotes is our raised spiritual discriminatory faculty; our fixed, unwavering, resolute divine intellect. Also, 'Be not afraid it is I' is referring to not being afraid of the bliss of our Christ presence within, to not be afraid to experience and express our divinity.

Meditation strengthens any other religious activities we may be involved in, for as it raises our soul-awareness level we begin to appreciate scriptural homilies more profoundly and we can relate to the texts with more understanding. (In the word 'religion', 're' means 'back' and 'ligion' means 'bind', so religion is meant to 'bind us back' to our creator, our inner spiritual roots.) We can now bring something really special to our places of worship and experience more deeply the divine presence. As we awaken, as Lazarus did, from the psychic sleep of the subconscious desert wilderness state, like coming out of winter hibernation, we begin to experience extraordinary clarity of being. We feel happier, livelier, more vital, like spring has sprung in our hearts, like we have fallen in love; we see love in everyone and everything and 'Love thy neighbour as thy Self' certainly rings true for us.

'As we wait (watch, meditate) in joyful hope for the coming of our Saviour Jesus Christ', we realise experientially that this 'coming', the second coming of Christ, is now, that this is already happening through our meditation as we 'watch with Me'.

My Heavenly Dear Friend

This perfect place to me I call
my heavenly dear friend,
its shade, its rays, they leave me, yes,
quite breathless now and then,
sometimes this view disarms my thoughts
and there's nowhere to hide;
just openness, a warm caress,
when I look into love's eyes.

A place of grace, a trance, a chance,
to glance is my delight,
for my soul it is attracted to
the sight of heaven's light
and there's nothing I can do or say,
just gaze in sweet surprise,
as all my cares just melt away,
when I look into love's eyes.

No beauty scene could recreate
a vision so serene,
for there is nowhere that can take
the place of love when seen;
a magic view, a world so true,
sure I've come to realise
that all my dreams are to be seen,
when I look into love's eyes.

These eyes erase my every doubt,
my heart feels it could fly,
among the stars that shine about
the velvet midnight sky.
Love's eyes embrace so joyfully
the treasured rainbow's end,
a silent dove just winging love;
my heavenly dear friend.

Suppression/Expression

Wherefore he saith,
awake thou that sleepest,
and arise from the dead,
and Christ shall give thee light.

(Ephesians 5:14)

Suppression is what we unconsciously do because of situations we have not consciously dealt with. We are not aware that we have not consciously dealt with them, so they become suppressed below our conscious level and thereby become subconscious. Suppression needs mental and physical tension to maintain its dynamic, so because of ignorance of present-moment awareness, suppression and its re-enactment – habitual reactions and reactive patterns – carries on in our lives uninterrupted. The subconscious automatically creates the tension that sustains suppression, the suppressed conditioning which, in itself, is the subconscious mind. Stress, anxiety and worry are needed to hold suppressed conditioning in place and out of conscious awareness. It is almost like a walking dream or psychic sleep, which we only become aware of the moment we awaken. Tension is the mask, the lid that covers suppression. Lift the lid on tension and suppression loses its dynamic, the subconscious begins to crumble and it becomes integrated into consciousness – awakened spiritual awareness.

If tension is the dynamic of suppression, then non-expression is the dynamic of depression. Expression is the opposite of depression. Every human being has the life force within their body, within their consciousness, and it needs to be brought to the surface and made conscious, i.e. expressed. The nature of this life force is intelligence –

67

blissful, loving, peaceful and creative – and as we express it through our being in our daily activities we become its nature in mind, body and spirit, benefiting the world as well as ourselves.

For example, let us say that one day this beautifully crystal-clear river is just flowing along, gurgling happily, simply expressing itself in perfect harmony with its surroundings. Then, one day, fear, worry, stress and tension develop and it becomes depressed. The river, or person, becomes as though cut off from the main flow of life – the life force – and becomes a dull, stagnant pool. Because of the lack of self-expression, of creativity, the lack of life force flow, depression becomes the state of mind.

Depression is like bliss turned inwards; expression through negativity, such as fear and anxiety. So, instead of experiencing the positive nature of bliss, of love, the person experiences the opposite. Depression is like deflated bliss, caused by lack of proper mental stimulation and outward expression of the person's true nature, which is bliss-consciousness – spiritual love.

When, through the regular practice of meditation, the physical nervous system gains the state of restful alertness then bliss becomes infused into the nature of the mind. This restful alertness, when the nervous system is neither active nor passive, is the dynamic through which bliss-consciousness is reflected within our consciousness; the mind becomes familiar with its own true nature. This process awakens us to the reality of God-consciousness within, thus imbuing the mind with divine wisdom.

With the presence of divine love in our heart now, we can readily identify that it was only suppressed fear, tension, anxiety, worry and the nature of all those negative forces that kept us rooted in depression; the state of ignorance – the non-experiential nature of bliss. We begin to acknowledge that the structure maintaining the suppression, which led to the depression, was only masked fear brought about by habitual ignorance.

'Perfect Love casteth out all fear'. Fear – conditioning, ignorance – being the opposite of love, is programmed by external influences into our consciousness and it denies the heart and mind the true nature of reality. Love, on the other hand, has its source from within; it is spiritual revelation, it is transcendental and it transmutes or dissolves all fear. Love is also beyond the man-made laws of opposites, like good versus bad, love versus hate, like versus dislike and all forms of duality.

Divine wisdom teaches that every moment is as is, that no moment or event can possibly come before any other moment or event and that every moment is perfect in its sequential order, regardless of our likes or dislikes, or whether, from the finite state of ignorance perspective, it was good or bad.

Regular meditation brings about the bliss-consciousness state, which becomes our permanent state of awareness. This state is also referred to as present-moment awareness or Christ-consciousness. During meditation, when we transcend, we enter into the causeless state, the non-relative state, the Eternal now; the state which is beyond time, space and causation. The Eternal now is within each being and its nature is bliss, which is revealed to us according to the degree of our purity, which evolves inherently through regular meditation practice. We don't need to remember bliss; instead, by giving birth to our Christ-consciousness through our inner virgin bliss-consciousness, we are automatically re-'membered' into the kingdom.

The only thing we need to remember is to meditate daily; indeed, these divine sittings could ideally be the highlights of our days. These blissful moments of utter silence, of wordless prayer, of being totally surrendered to the Spirit of God, for healing and purification, is what spiritual life and growth is all about. These are special times of reverence, when we give ourselves over entirely to individual contact with the divine – 'The Kingdom of God is within'.

The kingdom of God is within – within your consciousness – awakened bliss. Let us say the body is the end organ of the nervous system, the nervous system is the end organ of the mind and the mind, the full mind, is the end organ of the spirit, of God. In order for the mind to experience bliss, it is necessary for the physical nervous system to be cultured gradually through the restful alertness that occurs during meditation. Then, in order to make the state of bliss permanent throughout our daily lives, we need to resume normal activity after meditation. This inward and outward stroke of going into and coming out of meditation is important for refining our overall physiology. For the mind to have an experience there must be a corresponding state within the nervous system, so when the mind becomes blissful, the body, the nervous system and the senses become spiritually nourished. This whole process of becoming spiritualised in mind, body and spirit is the alchemy which transforms fear into love, suffering to bliss and suppression to expression.

Spirit of Confidence

The spirit of confidence, relaxation, flows through me now,
and through my natural and calm, relaxed self-expression,
the experience of confidence and relaxation manifests
even greater now within my consciousness.

As I express freely now my true and magnificent loving nature
I can experience the presence of deep inner strength and joy,
the wonder of my natural, happy, flowing confidence
rejuvenating and empowering my consciousness
of blissful self-esteem and confidence well-being.

As I express outwardly now this gleaming new
inner confidence and assertiveness,
I'm feeling renewed in love,
with a more positive and natural personality shining through,
leaving me feeling now abundantly more cheerful,
friendly and relaxed in my social activity, work and relationships.

As I relax, the greater the flow of well-being.
As I express my true nature, the greater my confidence.
And as is nature and all creation the supreme expression
of confidence,
so, too, am I, as its cherished and valued part,
this radiant, expressive channel,
this glorious and magnificent spirit of confidence, of
love, of bliss.

Subconsciousness

He restoreth my soul:
he leadeth me in the paths of righteousness
for his name's sake.

(Psalm 23:3)

Consider this saying by the Prophet Isaiah, 40:3 – 'A voice cries: in the wilderness prepare ye the way of the Lord. Make straight in the desert a highway for our God. Every valley shall be lifted up, and every mountain and hill be made low: the crooked shall be made straight, and rough places a plain: And the glory of the Lord shall be revealed, and all flesh shall see it together: for the mouth of the Lord has spoken.'

We shall return to the prophet's words later, but for now let us ask: what is the subconscious mind? Where is it? How did it get there? And how do we get rid of it? (Some inspirational writers refer to the subconscious as infinite being, spelling subconscious instead with a capital 'S' to denote Godhood. The subconscious referred to in this book is quite the opposite.)

In reality there is no such thing as the subconscious mind. It is not a separate mind as such, but rather the unconscious aspect of our full mind. It is like one-fifth of the iceberg above the surface representing our conscious mind, while the remaining submerged four-fifths represent the unconscious aspect of our full mind. We each have been given a full conscious mind, but it is we who separate this mind into conscious and subconscious.

Because of our conditioned state of ignorance, of the submerged four-fifths, which occurred when we hid ourselves from God, we have been living in 'this wilderness'; we have been put outside the Garden of Eden. This is illustrated by Adam disobeying God. Adam is symbolically credited with creating the first subconscious mind by hiding his spiritual nature from God.

To this day, we are still hiding from God when we each deny present-moment awareness. When we hide ourselves from the truth we make it an untruth, we live a lie, a falsehood, meaning that we are living either the past or the future. We hide from full consciousness through our ignorance and we make do with subconsciousness, thus creating separate identities for ourselves.

The subconscious state is the cause of all the suffering and misery that exists within the individual, nationally and globally. Scripture refers to this as 'and darkness prevailed the land'. Darkness is the subconscious; the land is the person's physical body and worldly affairs.

Fear is the driving force of the subconscious: living in the past, anxious about the future, being everywhere in our awareness except with God, in present-moment consciousness. By suppressing the present moment we give continuance to the subconscious. We refuse to acknowledge our mistake and we are forbidden entry into the Garden of Eden, bliss-consciousness, and in this way fear continues to dominate the heart and mind.

'Perfect Love casteth out all fear'; the solution from Jesus the Master. Perfect love is not an emotional state; perfect love is all that is, minus the subconscious, the conditioned state, our ignorance. It is not sufficient to seek perfect love, but rather to seek to eliminate the subconscious by way of integration. Perfect love is already present within, with us always as we journey out of the desert; 'Lo, I am with you even unto the ends of the world' (to the end of suffering). When we commence meditation, we are beginning the end of suffering whereby perfect love becomes our experiential nature. When we reclaim our full consciousness, then there is no subconscious agenda driving our daily living. Full consciousness is bliss-consciousness, when we are experiencing present-moment awareness through all our activities. When we are no longer recognising, being influenced by or consciously associating with the former conditioned state, it is like emerging from hibernation, from a psychic sleep. We only become aware we were dreaming the moment we wake up.

It is time for us to wake up and move onwards and upwards in our enlightened state, away from our addictive and reactionary nature, and to express instead, through our awakened spirit, the nature of God. We then cease making judgements on the present moment which, in reality, is perfect and which we have no right or need to judge.

'Forgive them Father for they know not what they do' is referring to operating from the reactive patterns of the subconscious mind. Every moment is perfect with God as author. It is only our state of subconsciousness, of darkness, of unreality, which we're looking through, that is the problem. Change our consciousness, change our world. This is the whole thrust of scripture; to raise our consciousness; 'Lift up your heart'. (The Bible generally refers to consciousness as the heart; hence 'Lift up your heart'.)

When Jesus healed the blind and the deaf, He lifted up their hearts; raised their level of consciousness, thereby eliminating the subconscious state. They could then see and hear from a higher state of consciousness. He restored them to wholeness of mind, body and spirit. They gave birth within their consciousness to new spiritual perceptions and understanding, reclaiming dominion over the desert, the wilderness of their subconscious and turning it into a garden of roses.

Another scriptural saying, 'The Truth shall set you free', seems, on the intellectual level, straightforward, but how do we relate to this as an everyday living truth with regard to the subconscious? What is the truth and what does it set us free from? Reading the word 'truth' and hearing it spoken is slightly different. When reading Truth we must be aware of the capital 'T' and not a small 't' as when hearing it. The Truth is our indwelling Christ, the bliss state within, the direct experience of present-moment consciousness. It sets us free from subconsciousness, perpetual ignorance and it raises our consciousness to spiritual life, Eternal life, union with the immortal heart of God: freed from the bondage of suffering, the subconscious mind.

Subconscious conditioning is also inherited and this is referred to biblically as original sin. St Peter, we are told, walked free from his prison when the guards fell asleep, symbolising when his conscious mind and thoughts were stilled. This freedom from the suffering state is a purification process and it can be brought about by meditation. We are then liberated from our prison and we become free in spirit. We then live through directly experiencing our bliss nature, present-moment awareness.

In the biblical story of when the people were invited to attend the wedding banquet, this was an invitation to enlightenment, to the kingdom of heaven. But one person was found to be not wearing a white garment and was refused entry to the banquet. The white garment symbolises the purified state, the state of self-realisation, and it can be attained at the present-moment awareness 'narrow gate' as in 'Enter ye at the narrow gate', for we are each invited to this wedding banquet. The present moment is the gateway to liberation from suffering, the elimination of the subconscious mind. Meditation thus ensures each of us the white garment by raising our consciousness. This white garment represents a complete transformation of consciousness, a synergy of full heart and mind expressing God-consciousness in unison and harmony, not only for our own good, but also our neighbour's and the environment at large. This is the glorious transformation of heart and mind that awaits all who seek freedom from subconscious conditioning, who seek to enter into bliss-consciousness, the kingdom.

Jesus said, 'The prince of this world cometh and findeth nothing in Me', when referring to His own state of consciousness; 'The prince of this world' being conditioning, ignorance of truth, which was not present within Jesus. And yet scripture says 'and they wrapped him in swaddling clothes', symbolising conditioning, which leads us to believe that Jesus, the man, in His formative years, had conditioning, too. So it is apparent that conditioning applies to all prior to self-realisation. This is why meditation practice is vital.

Reflect upon these words: 'And He descended into hell'. Hell represents the sinful, subconscious state of ignorance. This scriptural prayer-line reveals the essence of God's nature: love, healing, compassion, forgiveness, for all people. It is conscious contact with the Christ-light within which redeems our soul from the suffering state, the hell of the subconscious mind. As no one could possibly remember all their transgressions, when we enter into meditation it is the Christ-light within which heals and integrates the subconscious into conscious awareness. It is He, God, the Almighty power, who descends into the hell of our suffering, thereby causing a transformation of mind, body and spirit: the born-again spiritual being. We are crossing the threshold into His kingdom, to live His peace, love, happiness and prosperity; 'Thy Will be done'.

Returning to the Prophet Isaiah, 40:3 – in translation: 'A voice cries (Inner Christ): in the wilderness (subconsciousness) prepare ye the way of the Lord (expanding bliss-awareness). Make straight in the desert (purify the mind) a highway for our God (Enlightenment)'. The prophet is reminding us here to wake up from the psychic sleep of subconscious ignorance, to shed the wilderness state, for self-realisation. As the old order falls away, new holistic understanding unfolds and new spiritual consciousness emerges.

It's Love I Have No Doubt

I have heard the rippling sounds
of rivers as they flow,
and I have heard the din of spring
wing gently as she goes,
and I have listened to the breeze,
to whistling trees on high,
to glistening leaves and summer fields,
to songbirds as they fly.

And I have held the scented rose,
so gentle and so sweet,
each petal still it fills my soul;
a fragrance while I sleep.
I've even held the meadow flower
for hours though in a dream
and the vision I was holdin'
was a golden smile serene.

And I have strolled in early dawn,
when morn is fresh with dew,
I've ambled o'er still hills and dales
through vales and places new,
and often have I heard it said,
'forever is of bliss',
and I have held a moment pure,
sure time did not exist.

But when I feel this wave within
it fades all other sounds,
the echo of its harmony
rebounds so peacefully,
yes, when I feel such calm, somehow
this 'wow' I want to shout,
a moment fine, oh so divine,
it's love I have no doubt.

Conditioning

Yea, though I walk through the valley
of the shadow of death,
I will fear no evil:
For thou art with me;
Thy rod and thy staff they comfort me.

(Psalm 23:4)

Conditioning remains in place for as long as we remain in the state of subconsciousness. 'And they wandered in the desert ...' in search of the Promised Land, the kingdom, enlightenment – the Promised Land being the state of our pure-consciousness, the truth of our being. Conditioning is subconscious programming, accumulated through our ignorance, re-enacting automatically in our daily lives – living as if hypnotised in all of our actions and behaviour through this unrealised state. This hypnotic state is diffused only by conscious realisation of present-moment awareness; then the illusion ends and we wake up.

Conditioning covers over our true nature with a false persona, a mask, a personality created through our state of ignorance, driven by the egotistical self. People act out or role-play this seemingly normal behaviour, this imposed conditioning in which layers of sin were incurred over generations by societal mass conditioning. This state of automatic, unconscious behaviour persists throughout one's life and even more is added to, for as long as the subconscious aspect of mind prevails.

The way of dealing with this submerged conditioning, where fear, phobias, complexes and addictions are stored, is not to deal with them individually but rather to integrate these negative patterns of the

79

subconscious into conscious awareness. There is no need to name the phobias or to deal with each fear and anxiety separately, for they all have their roots in the same subconscious conditioning, referred to in the Bible as darkness or sin.

How, then, do we rid ourselves of darkness? Well, we shouldn't fight darkness or treat it with another form of darkness or ignorance; instead, we introduce light. This is how we deal with subconscious conditioning: we introduce awareness, light, which alone heals and restores, eradicating the darkness. It is light, pure-consciousness, which transforms the finite conscious mind into infinite omnipotent consciousness. The conscious mind is individual, but consciousness is universal – the 'all' mind, the whole mind – bringing coherence to the individual fragmented mind; the aspect which broke away, became subconscious and hid itself from wholeness, from God.

We do not try to do anything about the conditioned state – like trying to fix it from the outside as such – 'It is not I which doeth the healing but my Father which art in Heaven', but rather we introduce the practice of meditation. We are not focused on any specific area of our subconsciousness, but merely immersed in meditation, in light, which is bliss-consciousness. This process is automatic, becoming our moment-by-moment experiential awareness. With light present, darkness or ignorance cannot prevail and night gives way to dawn and suffering yields to bliss, to pure-consciousness. Meditation, like air and water, is neutral, beneficial and life-supporting to all humans. It is where all religions meet, bringing us, through integration and purification, into the light of God.

With the massive growth in spiritual awareness, in consciousness development – which is the path of the future evolution of mankind – there really is no need for continual suffering in the world today. It is this global rejuvenation, this expansion of spiritual consciousness, which ultimately will prevent wars and make them redundant, both individually and internationally. This will come about only when enough people have been awakened from their subconscious psychic sleep state into authentic awareness, into present-moment consciousness. It is time now to stop trying to conquer people and nations, to stop trying to advance for personal or national gain at the expense of others. Instead, let us conquer the real demon – the demon within ourselves – the plunderer of the human spirit, which is the small, egotistical, conditioned mind, the nature of which is only to maintain the status quo, the darkness state, the ignorance. This subconscious conditioning is the only real enemy to be eradicated. Get this right, and like a global family at peace, we will find ourselves back in the Garden of Eden.

Meditation as a practice for enlightenment and for the elimination of all personal suffering should be actively encouraged by governments and by those who carry influence in their society. The effect of how conditioning is imposed upon others and how it is propagated on a nation's citizens needs closer attention. Awareness campaigns relating to the impact of advertising should be made 'standard issue' to every citizen. People should be made aware of how conditioning through advertising insidiously influences the person and their unguarded innocence, especially very young people who, through ignorance of this, can live through years of suffering before they realise they had been programmed by advertising, by corporate and societal greed.

When the burdens of the world have been lifted from our shoulders through meditation practice, we realise that the cost of such ignorance, in terms of physical and mental health, has been great. Probably then, for the first time, the experience of youth starts flooding back, as the secret of youth and life prolongation is through consciousness development. A new order of awareness is born from within and a new generation of spiritual beings emerge. Meditation, by deconditioning age-old programmes, unfolds a state of youthfulness, of timelessness, into our consciousness, where we can feel perpetually young at heart. It rejuvenates the spirit from within, which is ageless and eternal – beyond time, space or causation. We become freed from the relative time-bound reactionary state of our ignorance for it is the Truth that has set us free. We have activated into conscious awareness the dormant nature of our true and everlasting state – bliss. Our search for peace of mind has ended, as love has now entered into our awareness and, by His Will, we are transformed, rejuvenated, into His nature, thereby getting to know, through direct experience, 'I am': God-consciousness within. Our inner and outer world now reflects present-moment awareness.

'Thy Kingdom come'. By this affirmation no longer are we searching, waiting, as through our meditation we become 'found' and this we are asserting, this moment. Through the mental stillness and through our surrendered ego struggle, the kingdom has come, for us, now. Out of the desert the kingdom has blossomed and our hearts reveal to us now this sacred state – transmutation through meditation; suffering to bliss.

With our hearts and minds now cosmically evolving through our newly enlightened state of spiritual perception we are thereby experiencing His life. The realisation is that God is love, that the love being expressed through us now, minus the conditioning, is God expressing His self, His divine order. Our conditioning is neutralised, we cease being reactionary and our raised consciousness now reflects His being – 'Lift up your hearts'.

We are now as His nature: light is our consciousness. When the lake is still and calm, when the storm, the conditioning, has been neutralised, when the nervous system has been reorientated and purified, then is the perfect Spirit reflected – 'Be ye also perfect as my Father in Heaven'. God within is released to play in our garden, He has found us as His friend, clear channels through which to express His evolutionary process, so that others may be inspired. We have been awakened unto love and we have been freed from the dream state of illusory experience to self-realisation, truth, reality; we have been freed from the bondage of subconscious conditioning to unbounded universal consciousness.

Searching

All we're searching for is love, true love,
to love our hearts cry out,
for I know when love it calls,
it will change our world about;
it will take just one embrace
to free love's wings within,
and we'll be lifted to that highest place
where happiness begins.

Love will take us to that paradise,
we'll be content once more,
we'll live each day the perfect way
in harmony I'm sure.
We'll be together, through all weather,
and what treasure we beget,
we'll thank all heaven for this blessing;
that our love-path we have met.

We'll be for all eternity
as rivers of the soul,
be free as we were meant to be,
our love be ever-flowin'.
Like beacons bright we'll fill the night;
our light to all be shown,
and share our love as nature does;
reflect what we have grown.

Integration

He rescued us from the power of darkness
and brought us safe into the kingdom
of his dear Son,
by whom we are set free, that is,
our sins are forgiven.

(Colossians 1:13–14)

The integrated person is one who has undertaken the process of conscious mind expansion, who has come out of ignorance of truth into enlightenment, into bliss-consciousness. The whole secret of the 'bliss' principle is integration. This means that at this stage we have use of our fully conscious mind, with no part taken over by subconsciousness. At this stage, we are free of addictive reactive patterns, the 'swaddling clothes' of the programmed, conditioned state.

Integration is at the subtle level, dealing with suppressions or addictions, some of which we may not even be aware of. We could be suppressing a past event, a fear, a phobia or deep-rooted anger towards someone or some situation. These suppressions or addictions are lived out either consciously or unconsciously; either by conscious, controlled participation or through denial, avoidance or unawareness of their existence.

In conscious addiction participation one surrenders the freedom of choice to say yes or no. It is compulsory, action-driven, from the subconscious. One partakes in the addiction consciously, with no power to override the automatic responses of the subconscious. It is this automatic response button that needs deactivating, by integration into consciousness.

Conscious avoidance, on the other hand, is suppression and it is a primary source of anger and stress build-up, which takes us out of the flow of full participation in life. It is unnatural, unfulfilling and contrary to Spiritual Law – the Life principle – which is to grow and expand happiness through self/soul-expression, not egotistical mind-expression, which is what the subconscious is. Thus, the whole cycle of one's life is dictated by suppressed reactive energy, which is the cause of all miseries, both individual and global. Integration is like peeling away the onion layers of suppressed reactive patterns and addictions, bringing about conscious mind expansion.

There is really no need to deal with individual problems or addictions, but rather to just infuse the mind with its own true nature, which is bliss. If the leaves on a tree are ailing the good gardener waters the roots. This enables the roots to draw in the necessary nutrients to travel to all the affected leaves simultaneously. It is an overall, holistic remedy and it is the same way that meditation works.

Integration is reclaiming and making whole and fertile the subconscious aspect of the mind. It is bringing life to the desert state within, purging the impurities and mental toxins of conditioning. This is, indeed, a blissful and joyous journey for those who undertake it; waking from the psychic sleep of ignorance into the light of life. For some, it is like falling in love for the first time and, in fact, we do, with our inner spiritual self, the nature of which is love. We begin to feel and see this love in all beings; 'Love thy neighbour as thy Self' (thy higher spiritual self). Through regular meditation, our state of spiritual awareness becomes permanent as we become transformed into unity-consciousness, one with the all, with God – chaos to cosmos.

No longer do we look through different coloured glasses at each separate person or thing, or fragment our present-moment awareness and filter this through the egotistical personality mind. Instead, having unmasked the false persona, the false, conditioned personality, we allow our true and magnificent, non-judgemental self-light to shine through. We see through reality as opposed to through illusion, the illusion of the false, unintegrated, subconscious mind. We see people and situations through a purified, spiritual clearness, rather than through our defiled collection of thoughts and opinions. We are 'experiencing' instead of judging.

Integration brings about peace of mind and contentment, which brings about the expansion of happiness, which is the purpose of life. We are consciously experiencing the power of God, prompting and guiding us through our daily situations; feeling full in heart and empty of egotistical, addictive routines. Intuitively, we are hearing the silent inner voice, deterring us from certain foods and harmful substances, such as alcohol, cigarettes and pharmaceuticals. Ignorance is replaced by wisdom. When this depth of awareness concerning unhealthy eating and damaging habits comes into effect, we know for certain that our meditation practice is paying spiritual dividends; that we are, indeed, on the royal road to an integrated life. By this process of integration, we expose ignorance and we make conscious the falseness, the illusion, of the jailer and the prison. We walk free. This is our victory march into the kingdom; our triumphant entry into Jerusalem, Christ-consciousness.

When the mind becomes familiar with its true nature, bliss, it no longer seeks lesser forms of happiness from outside sources. Instead, it is eternally content from within. Nothing of the senses, of the relative world, can substitute the state of bliss-consciousness, the elevated state of God-awareness. The soul has found its way home, it has become reunited with God, ending separation, and once there it will never relinquish this divine state to a lower evolutionary level. It will never devolve; only evolve to ever higher states of consciousness: 'In My Father's Kingdom there are many mansions'.

Integration of subconsciousness brings about such quality of spirit that our only real need, which is the need of the kingdom, is to express this out into the world in our daily lives. We will find this expression particularly fulfilling when with like-minded souls.

However, with less-evolved souls, although we can certainly offer guidance and assistance gladly and willingly, incompatibility, through the gulf of ignorance on the one hand, with the newly-evolved understanding on the other, will soon become obvious. This duality of awareness cannot easily coexist and it is the primary cause of marital and all kinds of relationship break-ups.

The nature of bliss is love, happiness, perfect health and prosperity: the spiritual ideal. All these divine qualities need expression through our spiritually awakened physicality. For this to be a real happening and not a contrived mood-making one, integration and purification of the nervous system has to be in process, so this is why we practice meditation. Purification is essential in order to express the spiritual ideal. With our newly-transformed state of spiritual awareness, thus are we ever manifesting the 'right hand of God', the will of God. God's divine plan for His kingdom is being brought about through us as His channel, His 'right hand'. The soul 'made in the image and likeness of God' raises man to this divine status.

This level of integrated spiritual awareness could be seen as the second coming of Christ, for it is, indeed, Christ-presence, living and unfolding through the individual soul for the betterment of mankind, spreading the good news that heaven is here for all, is within our raised consciousness and is easily attained: Christ is, indeed, risen, within us. Christ within has raised our spiritual vibration and has saved our soul from further suffering here on earth, from separation, ignorance. He has raised our soul to Eternal life, whilst inhabiting our physicality here on earth. Eternal life is then experienced and lived simultaneously within our relative state. The tombstone of subconsciousness has been rolled back and we are freed to soar in spirit, to express life into the world. 'Feed my children, feed my flock'.

St Peter, in the Bible, we are told, walked to freedom when the guards (his thoughts) fell asleep. When his conscious mind was stilled, his subconsciousness was integrated. Each person's prison is different in make-up, for its nature can be a concoction of many, or all, of the soul-destroying addictions that are common in today's society. We will each recognise our own prison, but from this hell can walk free, happily and triumphantly.

Our road to Damascus may be strewn with thorns, hardship and heartache, but once the process of dedicated, daily meditation has commenced, we begin to experience directly the power of God's forgiveness and healing. As enlightenment dawns within our consciousness, it seems as if everyone around us, and the whole world, changes, as we lose our different shades of glasses, our layers of conditioning. But in reality, it is we who have changed; it is we who have been transformed: water into wine. The process from separation to unity has begun, with full integration the assured outcome, not selective integration.

Intuitively, we begin to understand the philosophical meaning behind the scriptures. We grasp with more clarity of intelligence the insights intended and how they relate to our own living situations. Prior to enlightenment, words from the scriptures could be meaningless, as we only related to them literally and not spiritually, unable to decode the spiritual nectar, the life-saving message.

In time, with perseverance, meditation brings about self-realisation. We receive in consciousness, through self-referral, answers or solutions to whatever request we make of divine intelligence. 'Ask and ye shall receive'. The term 'waiting on God' becomes clear: that we serve God by living present-moment awareness. This divine awareness is now, for us, our only reality and higher states of divinity can now be graced to us. No longer are we tuned into a cacophony of stations, but into the clarity and purity of the divine transmitter: God. We are receiving directly from unified intelligence, the Principle, God, guiding and maintaining in perfect harmony and bliss all which His presence passes through: integrated consciousness.

When I'm Holding You

Love's the season my heart's in,
the harvest of my soul,
love's the reason why I can't conceal
this bright, sweet summer rose;
each moment speaks an essence deep,
fresh scented as the dew,
yes, there's a fragrance to my world You bring
when in my heart I'm holding You.

There are sparkling sights, romantic nights,
that take my breath away,
the magic when the moon is bright,
the stars in twinkle play;
a laughing maze of dancing shades,
a serenade to view,
yes, it's music to my world You bring
when in my heart I'm holding You.

There are moments, yes, oh heavenly blessed,
as the love in us it speaks,
and in all those ways which nature gave
to let us know of peace;
an ocean pound, a soul rebound,
deep echoes wild and true,
like the beauty to my world You bring
when in my heart I'm holding You.

Yes, whenever You are near it's clear,
my world it knows no time,
You touch my spirit tenderly,
each moment's so divine;
it's heavenly just You and me,
the sky seems always blue,
yes, it's summer to my world You bring
when in my heart I'm holding You.

The Word – The Mantra

In the beginning was the Word,
and the Word was with God,
and the Word was God,

(St John 1:1)

Everything in existence has its origin in the Eternal, vibrational love-silence of God – the creative silence. Ultimately, 'the Word' is cause and man is effect. 'The Word' is the dynamic, the vibrational silence sounded deep within our consciousness, which leads to self-realisation. It is not the hearing of multiple spoken words that brings about enlightenment, but rather silently hearing one vibrational word-sound within. It is not that we need to remember certain words, but we are just to hear, to be, with openness of mind. We are not building a memory bank of words and phrases, but we are seeking transformational soul-nourishment through 'the Word'. The spirit reveals itself in proportion to the openness and stillness of our conscious mind. Instead of several words, we can simply use just one word, with maybe a few syllables. In meditation, this is known as the mantra. As with all words, the essence of the mantra is vibrational, cosmic energy.

It is interesting to note how the 'a' or 'ah' sound is used throughout many spiritual traditions and particularly 'aum' in Eastern traditions, whence Christianity has its roots. In these traditions, the 'ah' vibration, which is the sound of happiness, of bliss, is in the character of words that are referring to, and are intended to mimic, the God sound or vibration, as in 'Gauud' or 'aum'. When recited in meditation it is not used with logical analysis but strictly for its vibrational, connective quality. The 'ah' sound/vibration is used for stirring the deeper levels of consciousness –

91

to make conscious through silent vibration that which is unconscious – to bring God-consciousness into our life.

In meditation, through the vibration of the mantra, sound goes from gross to subtle and from subtle to transcendent, like the merging of a single wave (finite mind) with the ocean (infinite mind.) It is the process of conscious contact with what already is – God-consciousness. The mantra is intended as a vibrationary communication means with the bliss principle – God – and it is this conscious contact which gives rise to the bliss experience. Thus, the mantra is the sound, the vibration, 'the Word' that awakens the inner Christ-child, the bliss-awareness state, which is normally kept asleep through the deafening, numbing, noise of the world of our thoughts. Paradoxically, it is now silence which awakens us.

The quote at the start of this chapter is a most powerful invitation to enlightenment. The practice of meditation brings us into direct communication with the nature of 'the Word', which alone can give us full contentment of heart – coming into the full stature of Christ or coming out of the darkness into the light. Spiritual rejuvenation or self-realisation is a complete 360-degree turnabout from that state which caused our darkness, our suffering. Mere intellectual knowledge of spiritual matters does not alter the state of the soul, only the direct experience of bliss can. Talking or thinking about an apple does not provide its taste; we have to bite into it to experience its juice and benefits. Direct communication with God is through the sound vibration of 'the Word'. When the heart and mind are pure and clear of conditioning our vibration level, our aura, is raised, is heightened spiritually, and is reaching God, remembering that God receives, and we can only perceive Him through present-moment awareness. The Spirit does not know past or future, for these are actually illusory states of mind.

In places of worship and religious paintings this vibrationary state is depicted over or around the heads of holy people as a circle, a halo, which represents their clear, bright aura portraying their raised consciousness. And so it is for each of us today – we are invited, through our 'Word', our sound, our mantra, to raise our consciousness and clear our aura. This is our real work in life while in the physical body on this earth plane – to seek self-purification, give birth to the Spirit, through self-awareness. Far from being a difficult and complicated process, this is easily achieved through daily meditation, although in order to ensure the proper practice it is advisable to learn from a qualified teacher. The mantra, 'the Word', is like a pebble dropped into a lake – the ripples it creates, like waves of bliss, vibrate and expand ever outwards, bringing consciousness to the entire lake. As we advance with our meditations, these ripples extend more and more into the deeper levels of the mind, awakening it consciously to its true nature – bliss.

We are now accessing the submerged continent of spiritual love awareness, which was denied to us experientially when we were put outside the Garden of Eden owing to our ignorance. This unconscious continent is comprised of non-integrated situations and happenings, which came our way in life and which were not dealt with consciously, in full spiritual awareness – when we were not in the present moment. These suffering situations were filed under 'the past', to be relived over and over until integrated through self-awareness. This, indeed, is the suffering zone, but our release is assured through the use of the mantra in meditation.

In meditation practice the mantra is not pounding away like a woodpecker at the bark of a tree, for that would amount to effort, whereas this process should be effortless. Neither are we trying to give ourselves a particular experience, direct what happens or control our thoughts and senses – attempt to become thoughtless. Rather, when we drift from the mantra we simply and gently return to it, for its purpose is to still the mind so as to expand conscious mind into subconscious mind – to bring into conscious awareness the vast, submerged continent of bliss. This purification is the elimination of the subconscious mind toxins through the process of entering into transcendental silence.

The soul has all the attributes of God Eternal, with the exception of bliss, so this is why, in order for the soul to 'know' the experiential nature of bliss, it must have conscious contact with the spirit within. And this contact, once gained, will grow, expand and strengthen the soul's capacity to know bliss permanently – for it to become our eternal experience. The mind, through mental stillness, needs to sink and submerge into the spirit within to come upon the bliss experience, which is the purpose of every soul's journey, is its liberation, our highest evolutionary point – bliss-consciousness, Eternal union. The use of 'the Word', the mantra, during meditation brings about the integration of soul-conditioning. This daily practice of letting go is vital for spiritual growth and soul evolution.

The Bible says 'and they (society) wrapped him in swaddling clothes (subconscious conditioning) and laid him in a manger'. Our upbringing, parental and educational influences, societal status, even national identity, are all forms of 'swaddling clothes'. It is as if swathed in spiders' threads of conditioning and attachments. When we consider attachments, an emotional intensity usually accompanies them. If, for instance, we are filled with superstition, jealousy, fear, anger or resentment regarding people, places, situations or possessions, then these negative emotions bind us and keep us attached to the very same that we long to be free of. This is our bondage, the state of ignorance of self. We need to free the soul from the disempowering 'swaddling clothes' to the empowering bliss-nature of Christ-consciousness. The soul cannot know bliss experientially while 'wrapped in swaddling clothes', but 'the Truth – the Spirit, shall set it free' – the vibration of 'the Word' shall set us free through its spiritually dynamic silence.

The 'manger' where the child was laid symbolises an ordinary person like you and me. He wasn't born in a palace as one would expect for such a special coming, but born in a stable, which represents the lowest and most deprived and troubled soul; the unworthiness they might feel. 'For unto us a child is born' – the virgin in the Bible symbolises the soul seeking God, the spiritual solution, through which the Christ-child, the Son of God, is born unto us, unto our own inner virgin-consciousness. He came to save the world, not the planet as such, but our own personal world. This miracle child, when matured through constant devotion and expression, is none other than God Himself. This miracle child then, in turn, takes care of the mother, the virgin soul, by acquainting it with its true nature – Eternal bliss. This results in true soul-peace, true union with God. The birth of the Christ-child within is the 'miracle' for each of us and everything consequent to this is miracle-consciousness, bliss-consciousness, which continues to manifest throughout our moment-by-moment, everyday living.

Every person has the Christ-child within, although other traditions may call it by different names. In any case, we each have to make conscious contact with it – give birth to our own inner child, our own spiritual awareness, for it to grow and expand in wisdom and strength. This results in true faith, which manifests our highest intentions through our creative aspect – God's will. In our highest state we are each 'made in the image and likeness of God' and so are capable of achieving dreams and aspirations far greater than the finite (unrealised) mind can fathom. We each have the power of this Christ-child within to change our lives, make new, manifest whatever we may conceive of through our miracle-consciousness, and the conscious contact is made during meditation, through the use of 'the Word', the mantra.

Beloved Jesus

Most blessed and beloved Jesus,
in the spirit now of loving thanks
I offer, Lord, my soul in praise.
Accept me as thy servant channel,
creating peace, serve thy name.
Release within me acts of kindness,
deeds of patience, words forgiving.
Guide my steps to quench a thirst,
serve from well of Spirit grace.

Most blessed and beloved Jesus,
cleanse me in my way of thinking,
purify my inner thoughts.
Plough within me depth of peace,
sow my heart with seed of love.
Speak the wisdom of Thy way,
open to me paths of love.
Forever be my guiding light,
Thy Spirit perfect shines Eternal.

Silence

Let us have confidence, then,
and approach God's throne,
where there is grace.
There we will receive mercy
and find grace to help us
just when we need it.

(Hebrews 4:16)

What is silence? Is it something that exists separately from noise? How do we interpret silence? Do we think we can only experience it in beautiful countryside?

There is relative silence and there is absolute silence. What is the difference? We usually define silence as the absence of noise. This is relative silence. Some of us try to avoid this silence by filling it with sound or mental chatter and sometimes we compare different relative sounds to decide upon the depth and quality of silence. But can we compare early morning birdsong or a rippling mountain stream to a rock concert?

Surely the greatest gift that God has bestowed upon mankind is the capacity to develop and experience transcendental pure silence within our being, within our hearts and minds. This divine silence is absolute silence, a state which is not of this world, not relative, as Jesus said, 'My Kingdom is not of this world.' It is within, within our consciousness.

Transcendental silence is the immutable Eternal pure silence of being. Being means just to be. Experientially, transcendental silence or being is bliss-consciousness which, when developed through regular meditation, exists simultaneously within our relative state, our everyday affairs. We make it conscious to the mind, for it is the true nature of the mind. Thus, some of us live our heavenly state unconsciously through ignorance. Transcendental silence is lived as awakened spiritual being. It is the alive, dynamic, Eternal presence, the kingdom which Jesus refers to as 'Father'. It is existence itself. It is God.

Let us consider the word, the sound, 'Ma-Ra-Na-Tha', a mantra which is used worldwide, meaning 'come, Holy Spirit' or 'come, Lord'. When spoken, we hear this with our ears, in its gross form, but when we repeat it in our head during meditation, the audible sound diminishes, until eventually our ears no longer perceive it. At this point, we continue to just 'think' the sound, as opposed to think 'about' it, singularly, with conscious awareness, perceiving it through the hearing sense silently within, until it reaches its quietest, subtlest state, when we become no longer aware of it. When it has thus serenely disappeared out of sensory range, this is transcendental silence, absolute silence, as opposed to worldly, relative silence.

The individual mind has now transcended the relative state of time, space and causation, the world as we know it, and it has arrived at the state of pure-consciousness, pure silence, bliss-awareness. Different traditions and religions use various words to describe this state, but the descriptive word is not the essence for, more importantly and undeniably, it is the experience that is the essence. When we have direct experience of transcendental silence it is a reality beyond the dogma. Experiencing takes us beyond the intellectualising of God and it gives us presence, reality, freedom. Belief and love take on new meaning and depth. We come to understand belief and silence to be one and the same reality, a state of being, love-silence belief; inner awareness.

In meditation, when experiencing bliss silence, there is nothing of our conditioned mind to compare, to voice opinions or to make judgements. We are not 'thinking about' God; how He should be or not be. Transcendental silence is where all religions meet, where there is no longer the need for signposts, although they served us truthfully and directed us to our 'home', where we are now at one with God. Coming out of meditation we bring God's presence within us into our daily lives. We don't need to continue to remember God as such, but rather our divine silence in action is our remembrance. Intellectual discrimination of reality satisfies the mind, but not the heart. Direct experience through meditation satisfies the heart.

So many people remain unaware intellectually, or experientially, of divine silence, comparing silence only with levels of sound or tranquillity; relative silence. Divine silence, absolute silence, is authentic awareness, our natural, inner spiritual state, our real home. This quality of heart and mind needs to be developed into consciousness. It is the medium through which we, in our finite state, develop and evolve into God-consciousness. To live this state of supreme awareness permanently is the purpose of life and the purpose of meditation. As beautiful as the countryside is, we don't have to be there in order to enjoy peace and quiet, for once the capacity to experience our natural state within is developed we can be in bliss silence anywhere, anytime.

The human nervous system is the most highly evolved of all God's creations on this earth and it is what separates mankind from the other life forms. We are so privileged, each of us having the opportunity to raise our consciousness to God-consciousness. As individuals, through the agency of our nervous system, senses and intellect, we can each progress to the full stature of Christ-consciousness. We have been granted the gift of the limitless capacity to expand in transcendental bliss silence while on this earth plane. This is our true vocation in life, our calling to divinity, which the Gospels are urging us towards: from water into wine, from suffering to bliss.

That which people, through ignorance, happily wish to avoid, is the very thing we vitally need to explore and come into conscious contact with more and more, not less and less. Divine silence, when matured through meditation, becomes and remains our permanent state of being, not just in places of tranquillity, but in every moment, and once attained it is not relinquished. Consciousness flows through the heart, so mature silence is love-consciousness, divinity made conscious within the mind.

At first, the experience of inner transcendental silence may be fleeting, but through finding the gap in the conveyor belt of our thoughts, it widens into longer periods, until we eventually come into unity-consciousness. If we hand over our every need to this unified field of intelligence, our source, it will work our lives out perfectly: 'Give us this day our daily Bread'.

This elevated state is the Sacred Heart within, knowing only love, compassion, peace and harmony, and all we have to do is make conscious contact with it through meditation for it to become our conscious state.

Mental stillness creates conscious mind expansion, which is transformational; indeed, life-changing. Instinctively, like salmon heading upstream, we are each seeking our birthing point: that place where we can give birth to our inner Christ-child through our virgin-consciousness. The long journey of the soul through the wilderness, the desert, of our ignorance, grief and suffering is coming to an end through the alchemy of transcendental silence. Through the power of absolute silence, the subconscious aspect of our full mind, which has been the cause of the suffering, surrenders its stronghold over our spirit unto the power of Christ.

Many seek this silence through nature, by walking in a forest or along a beach, or through visiting churches or going on retreats, all of which I have done and still do, but wherever enlightened divine silence may be first experienced, thereafter its presence will always be our guiding force. Never tiring of the Lord's work as we perform divine actions, all our expressions become devotional silence in praise and honour of God, as Jesus said, 'I must be about My Father's business.'

Once we commence the practice of meditation we begin to value more deeply the previously incomprehensible; the God-given status that gives us the capacity to enter into our full, conscious mind through gaining purity of the subconscious. Now we understand why Jesus asks us to 'Enter ye at the narrow gate', for this 'narrow gate' is the gap in our thoughts, the entry point back into paradise, into His nature, while we are still at the same time in our relative state.

His nature becomes our nature, whence come all our manifestations of creativity, prosperity and perfect health. 'Man', in manifestation, denotes that as spiritual beings, mankind is intended to manifest God's intentions, as in 'By their fruits shall ye know them'. We are each 'created in the image and likeness of God' to manifest His nature through self-expression. His nature can only become known to us through the purity of our consciousness, which is gained in transcendental silence. We then become aware of our God-given talents and as we express them, they multiply and we experience inner silence as the 'flow of life'.

By now, we should be understanding that absolute silence is a profound state of being rather than the mere absence of noise, that it is transcendental, not of this world, not relative, and it can be brought to conscious awareness by direct experience through meditation; that it is the medium through which our inner reality unfolds to us, it is the dynamic, spiritual force behind all of creation, it is the essence of our being and its nature is bliss.

Spiritual beings and silence beings are one and the same. Our inner spiritual world is developed through pure silence and it is the physical nervous system, which is the end organ of the mind, which facilitates this. The human nervous system, the most evolved on this earth, is the physicality through which pure silence is made to manifest, experiential to the mind. For the mind to experience anything there must be an equivalent state in the nervous system. The process of bringing the nervous system to restful alertness during meditation, then back to normal activity, is what brings about its healthy functioning and ensures the full infusion of bliss into the nature of the mind; the full integration of optimum brain activity; left and right brain coordinating in unison, in higher brain consciousness; the five senses of perception operating at their maximum potential. Once cultured, dynamic silence, bliss-consciousness, remains our permanent state of awareness, of self-referral. We are influenced and guided by the laws of nature, natural law, living in accordance with this cosmic awareness.

At this stage, divine inner silence is experienced as belief. Pure silence is belief itself, perfect belief; enlightenment. Pure-consciousness does not require someone or something to believe in, as this would put the power outside of us. Belief-consciousness is inherent in the deep, inner silence of meditation. Once purity is gained, belief is automatic;

it is an attitude of heart, becoming present in all our goals and activities. Our objectives then conform to the natural evolutionary process, the will of God. Our needs become the needs of nature.

Transcendental silence evolves our finite mind to infinite mind, union with God, from existing to existence. Existence is pure Eternal-consciousness and this spiritual capacity is within all human beings, regardless of our past actions. We are invited into the Kingdom of God, heaven, but we're reminded through scripture that we must be of a purified state of soul, 'wearing a white garment', which is achieved through absolute silence. This is the purpose of meditation.

Reflection

Visible sky of day and night,
reflection of the state,
surrendering fully to the dawn,
dispelling darkness certain.

Allowing life express through me,
receiving light, spreading truth,
radiance, from awareness
of greater power than I.

Each tree and rose designed at seed,
firmly rooted in the source,
growth unhindered by distraction,
of single duty for to bloom.

This path for me, divine in nature,
gives fullness of my purpose,
uncovering the essence, the love,
such promise of the blossomed spirit.

Summer meadows act as witness,
exposure of design,
fulfilment of the asking,
for beauty to be shown.

In this state of oneness,
of guidance to be true,
I hear the soundless calling,
my answer to be seen.

Expand my beam, radiate,
expression from within,
beauty for release,
reflection of the light.

Living our Bliss

He that dwelleth in the secret place of the most High
shall abide under the shadow of the Almighty.
I will say of the Lord, He is my refuge and my fortress: my God;
in him will I trust.

(Psalm 91:1–2)

Bliss resides transcendentally within the silence of the heart, invisible yet present, like the vapour of the ocean, which only through contact with the sun becomes visible. Likewise, bliss, like the ocean, needs conscious contact for it to become experiential. Living our bliss, or living the Spirit, can also be likened to a musician playing music through their instrument – the physical body in awakened consciousness – and the music being the life situations: family, relationships and work. The sound quality of our music, meaning the quality of our life experiences, our bliss, is in direct proportion to our purified consciousness, our mind expandedness.

Living our bliss is always spontaneous action through present-moment awareness of what we are actually doing through our five senses – paying full attention to what we are seeing, hearing, smelling, tasting and/or touching at the time. We are fully experiencing the happening-nature of our action or non-action – our intellect, our thought, always remaining steady, resolute, in dealing only with the moment and the activity or non-activity. This is living meditation.

Resolute intellect, which is the result of regular meditation, is focused power of attention, our sense of 'I'-ness, 'I am'-ness, the 'I' established and functioning as the self – 'Be not afraid it is I' – our own indwelling Christ, our inner self. Established resolute intellect is being in the cosmic moment; it is the mastery of our minds and senses and it is a state of Eternal peace – the highest state of human evolution. Only the transcendent self within can master the senses, not the small egotistical 'I'. The senses can never be mastered by a conscious effort; it is transcendental silence through meditation which purifies.

The purpose of meditation, then, is to bring us to established intellect, whereby our senses cease 'wandering in the desert' of ignorance, seeking random, worldly pleasures to satisfy the unrealised mind and senses. The unrealised mind is in constant demand for any forms of relative 'happiness' and it finds this readily through the unpurified, unawakened senses, which rob us of intellect, thus keeping the mind and senses anchored in addiction and time. After meditation, when the mind re-emerges into the relative world, it is infused with cosmic bliss and life is then lived and experienced through purified sensory activity – the instrument and music perfectly in tune, in perfect harmony. The nervous system, through which we experience our senses, is the seat of consciousness and during meditation the breath and the metabolism reach their lowest point when in the transcendent state. Cosmic bliss-consciousness is made permanent through the constant cycle of meditation, then activity – normal living – then meditation and so on.

Unconditional love is another way of describing this state of living our bliss, where the mind is congruent with nature, is in 'made-up' mode; is of resolute intellect, while dealing non-judgementally from the heart with whatever else is happening. This is when we let every situation, every moment, pass effortlessly through our conscious awareness without judging whether we like or dislike what is happening, always remembering that every moment is perfect, until contaminated by anger, fear or judgemental thinking – 'judge not lest ye be judged'. In this way, the bliss nature of the situation, the moment, the pure music, is expressed through our conscious awareness, the instrument, with all its purifying and healing benefits, extending further out into the universe to continue its perfect vibrational effect.

Meditation also activates, or awakens, the seven spiritual centres, or chakras, within the body, most significantly the pineal and pituitary glands located in the upper head area which, when awakened, channel the Spirit of Christ. The pastoral crozier, the staff, represents the spiritual centres and the crook of the staff represents the pineal and pituitary glands. This is how, when awakened, these two spiritual centres become the body and blood of Christ and we say that we 'eat' His body and 'drink' His blood, meaning we live and experience His bliss through our raised spiritual consciousness. This is true Holy Communion: living in Christ unity-consciousness – living our bliss.

Perfect Melody

The music of true love, is there in everyone,
a tune that beats of peace eternally;
A song for us to know, like rivers ... it must flow,
this chant will touch the hearts of you and me;

We hear it in the street, wherever people greet,
we hear it through sweet nature's family;
A splendour of the soul, a wonder to behold,
a miracle just waiting to be free.

When skies are not so blue, when clouds are passing through,
echoes of this tune are there to cheer;
Like waves upon the sea, in ocean harmony,
a choir of peace so good for us to hear;

When life is calling out, when change is all about,
this music chimes so beautifully;
With every note revealed, such joy the heart it feels,
these simple scales are tuned so perfectly.

So let us take this song, let us make the chorus long,
let us sing it to the world in harmony;
Let us sing it concert clear, let us make it, oh, sincere,
for love is just the perfect melody.

World Peace through Natural Law

Blessed is the man that walketh not in the counsel of the ungodly,
nor standeth in the way of sinners,
nor sitteth in the seat of the scornful.
But his delight is in the law of the Lord;
and in his law doth he meditate day and night.

(Psalm 1:1–2)

Throughout the chapters of this book, metaphysical words and phrases are used frequently, such as enlightenment, bliss, present-moment awareness, heightened awareness, expanded awareness, authentic awareness, spiritual awareness, cosmic awareness, raised consciousness, Christ-consciousness, God-consciousness, divine presence, divine nature, true nature, truth, inner child, inner self, self-realisation, reality ... These all comprise the single primeval understanding: the unified field of natural law, which is the immutable transcendental silence of which all activity of the relative plane – past, present and future – has its origin. Natural law is that which governs the entire physical universe, from the hair on our heads to the grass in the fields, from the blood in our veins to the flowing rivers. From its unchanging Eternal status it governs and maintains us and nothing can exist without the presence of natural law. Its laws, which are God's laws, are perfect and transgressions are proportionate and inescapable; hence, ignorance leads to suffering. Doesn't it make so much sense, now that we know the cause of suffering, to pay attention to this, to do something about it – to do the inevitable – to attune our consciousness with natural law.

The secret for us humans to live happily, healthily and prosperously is to harness the intelligence, the organising power of nature – the

109

unified field of natural law. Law and Lord are the same, the same power: God, the author of natural law which regulates the universe, the cosmos. Meditation brings our mind into conscious attunement with natural law and no matter what our religious practice, natural law will be at its core, although the words to describe it may differ. There is no escaping the undeniable truth that we each, as human beings, have our origins in natural law; our real home, which exists only in the now or present-moment consciousness. All devotion in silence automatically attunes with natural law and to know peace of heart and mind we must first experience transcendental silence.

When one considers the defence budget of the world's most economically powerful nations, the mind surely boggles. The world and the human mind, for many, have not evolved much beyond the pollution of ignorance: fear, greed and addiction. It is beyond comprehension that the superpowers fail to see the futility of trying to evolve economically and spiritually through fear and domination, because it can never, ever work. The essence of the human spirit is love and compassion, which are the same, so any other type of expression can only warp and degrade the human mind into a subcultural existence and thus to suffering; devolving rather than evolving. For a mere fraction of their defence budgets, these nations could insulate themselves against terrorism, greed and the need for war by simply introducing meditation programmes into their educational systems. This would ultimately lead to a unified diversity consciousness, having the effect of making it impossible for anyone, personally, locally or internationally, to want to dominate, overthrow or injure another soul. Surely this is the intention and aim of every person and nation, deep down, to know heaven on earth, both within and without.

This, indeed, makes practical sense and it would portray great leadership qualities of the heads of nations, who constantly express concern about national and international peace. World peace starts with the individual and as such is every person's responsibility, but governments need to take the initiative through awareness campaigns and not just leave it to private meditation groups to create national and international coherence. World peace will not come into being through worldly consciousness – 'My Kingdom is not of this world'. This is why, through meditation, we need to alter our worldly consciousness into transcendental consciousness; natural law consciousness. What is needed is a unified coexistence of all cultures, by becoming cosmically evolved beings through consciousness development. This would guarantee local, national and international coherence and it would eliminate forever the need for war – a global state of consciousness, beyond all religions, within all peoples, prospering and empowering each individual and each nation through natural law; the one and only law that we each have our being in and which we need to be consciously attuned with.

Let us create peace in the hearts and minds of the world's citizens by setting up meditation groups. Let us be sincere in taking the necessary steps to ensure personal, national and global peace on this wonderful planet, this potential paradise that we each call home, and whose bounties should benefit all peoples and all nations. The human spirit, when expressed purely, in whichever culture, creed or denomination, has no equal or rival. There is nothing of this world that we can conceive of that can lift more readily, individually and nationally, to the state of exhilaration, love and compassion than the human spirit in full bloom. This state exists within each person already, but it just needs to be brought forth by tapping into the unified field of natural law – the real and effective way of securing perfect health, prosperity and world peace for all.

His Day

Oh, His day is divine and through His magical time
created bright stars of light spans,
whitewashed ocean seashells, scent meadows bluebells,
and set each to His purposeful plan.
For each soul it is so, that our hearts they may know
the great promise to all that ring true,
some wind and some rain, even rugged terrain,
then that cloud's silver lining's bright hue.

Yes, His day is for all, that heavenly call
to witness, to love and to prayer,
with all of our being, through quiet moments serene,
can we each our true nature declare.
Oh, His day is such joy, His day won't deny
all the peace a still moment can bring,
from His silence within, let His presence begin
to raise up our hearts on high wings.

Yes, His day is for love, His day is all good,
His day offers all vision and hope,
with freedom and fun, in love-faith, everyone
growing stronger in wisdom and scope.
Then evening is sent, oh this precious event,
all our toils for to rest for a while,
yet, His day it lives on, preparing the dawn,
for new morn's pure-sweet, glorious smile.

Bibliography

New Testament, Good News Edition, The Bible Society (1987)

The Holy Bible, Authorised King James Version (1958)

The Holy Bible, New Revised Standard Version, Anglisized Edition (1989-1995)